NOT ALL
HEROES
WEAR
CAPES

To the wonder and marvel of ordinary people living ordinary lives. – NB

First published in Great Britain in 2020 by Wren & Rook

ISBN 978 1 5263 6289 6

10 9 8 7 6 5 4 3 2 1

Wren & Rook
An imprint of
Hachette Children's Group
Part of Hodder and Stoughton
Carmelite House
50 Victoria Embankment
London EC4Y 0DZ

An Hachette UK Company
www.hachette.co.uk
www.hachettechildrens.co.uk

Publishing Director: Debbie Foy
Editor: Phoebe Jascourt
Art Director: Laura Hambleton
Designer: Tina Garcia

Printed and bound in China

The website addresses (URLs) included in this book were valid at the time of going to press. However, it is
possible that contents or addresses may have changed since the publication of this book. No responsibility
for any such changes can be accepted by either the author or the publisher.

NOT ALL

HEROES

WEAR

CAPES

BEN BROOKS

ILLUSTRATED BY **NIGEL BAINES**

wren
&rook

What Is a Superhero?

'A HERO CAN BE ANYONE, EVEN A MAN DOING SOMETHING AS SIMPLE AND REASSURING AS PUTTING A COAT AROUND A YOUNG BOY'S SHOULDERS TO LET HIM KNOW THE WORLD HADN'T ENDED.'
– Batman

I want you to picture a hero. Who are you imagining? Someone who can fly? Turn invisible? Lift a car off someone with just their little finger? Someone in an uncomfortable-looking costume and an expensive-looking car?

Most people don't think they're heroes. In fact, even after people do incredibly brave things, they'll often say something like: 'I'm not a hero, I'm just an ordinary human being'.

This made me wonder what it actually means to be a 'hero'. Can an ordinary human be a hero too? Could I ever be a hero? What about you?

Before I wrote the book you're holding now, I wrote about the lives of three hundred different people for a series of books about individuals who dared to be different. Each person was chosen because they did, said, sang or made something that improved the lives of those around them. Some of them made discoveries among the stars, some put their lives on the line for peace, some raised money for those less fortunate than themselves and others spread joy through music, literature or art.

To me, each of those people were heroes. Why? Well, **I would define 'hero' like this:**

A HERO
is someone who
WANTS TO LIVE
in a better world
and decides
TO DO SOMETHING
about it.

That's the definition I believe to be true, at least. If you look 'hero' up in the dictionary, it might say something slightly different, but this isn't a dictionary, it's my book and I get to decide what it says. (It could say 'pizza is a vegetable' or 'headlice make good pets' if I wanted it to, though I'll try to keep things as close to the truth as possible.)

The cape-wearing superheroes in our films and comics still fit nicely into this definition: they want to make the world a better place and they all try to do something about it. Whether they were born with supernatural powers or slowly developed their abilities through painstaking practice, heroes try to help others whenever they get the chance. Batman wants to rid Gotham of crime. Black Panther protects Wakanda. Superman clears crooks off the streets of Metropolis. Wonder Woman even seems to spend a lot of her time fighting in the Second World War.

⚡ BUT NOT ALL HEROES WEAR CAPES. ⚡

And our world is filled with people like this, too. They may not leap between buildings or soar through clouds, but that doesn't mean they haven't devoted their lives to making the world a kinder, safer, better place. They have found and developed skills, passions, talents and beliefs, and these become the 'superpowers' which they use to help others. Some spend their free weekends running marathons to raise money for charity. Others feed the homeless on the streets of their cities. A few dive into caves to rescue trapped children. Some children grow and cut off their own hair to make wigs for people who have lost theirs. Others notice someone at school being bullied and decide to stand up for them.

There are so many ways we can be forces for good that almost every passion, talent, interest, knowledge, strength or skill can be put to use. Whether you want to rescue llamas, end bullying, discover vaccines, cook for the hungry or play the trombone for those who need cheering up, I hope there's something in this book that will inspire you to find your superpower and use it for good.

Since learning about the lives of so many people, I've become much better at quizzes than I was before, I can tell you who invented earmuffs, and I know what year the first plane took to the skies.[1] But more importantly than that, I've started to understand what it means to be a hero.

This book is my attempt to tell you what I've learned. Along the way, I want to introduce you to some of my heroes. Most of them aren't particularly famous. Most of them think of themselves as ordinary people. But all of them have done extraordinary things.

If you're anything like me, you might sometimes feel quite daunted while reading about the lives of so many incredible people. How do I compare? you might be thinking. How will I ever join the ranks of those amazing people? The good news is that you don't have to be like those people, you just have to be like you. Which is lucky, because ...

no one is more like you than you are.

And once you've settled on just being you, you can get to work on honing your superpowers. It doesn't matter how big or small they are, it only matters that you use them to make a difference, whether it's by helping a stray cat, a member of your family, your school, your country or even your entire planet.

Over the next few pages, I hope to prove that you are as capable of changing the world as any of the people we're about to meet. You exist, you're you, and you're holding this book in your hands. That's all you need to get started.

[1] Earmuffs were invented by Chester Greenwood when he was just fifteen, and on December 17th 1903 the Wright Brothers made the first flight in their plane.

DARE TO DREAM

1

'SHOOT FOR THE MOON, EVEN IF YOU MISS, YOU'LL LAND AMONG THE STARS.'
- Norman Vincent Peale

When I was around half the size I am now, I spent most nights secretly reading under my duvet by the light of my phone. I'd found a book called *Heroes of Polar Exploration* at a jumble sale. The book told the stories of people venturing to the coldest places on earth and, quite often, dying in them. These early explorers battled to survive in treacherous lands as they tried to gather scientific data on forces never before encountered by humans. Their toes froze and fell off, they starved, they started to see things that weren't there and many spent years lost in the icy wilderness. I was obsessed.

Soon, I was reading all I could about Antarctica and the Arctic. I spent my free time drawing maps. I planned expeditions across ice shelves and learned the different parts of a ship. When I read that Ernest Shackleton survived a polar winter by eating his dogs, I asked myself whether I too would eat my dog if I became an explorer. (I decided I wouldn't and that I'd just try and remember to bring enough cheese and onion crisps to last the whole journey.)

I have since found out that discovering your passion between the pages of a book is quite common. Written words can set off ideas in the imagination that might persist for our entire lives. Take Joanne Liu, for example:

Joanne was thirteen when she read a book about a man working for an organisation called Médecins sans Frontières (MSF) in Afghanistan.[1]

Joanne thought about that doctor working all by himself in the lonely mountains. She thought,

this is the kind of meaning I'd like to have in my life.

[1] MSF (also known as Doctors Without Borders) is a group of doctors who offer medical help to whoever in the world needs it most, regardless of who or where they are. This often means working in dangerous war zones, places that have been devastated by natural disasters and countries in which deadly diseases are spreading.

Joanne studied hard at school and became a doctor. Nearly twenty years after she'd first read that book, Joanne joined MSF. She has since helped countless victims of disasters, wars, famines and diseases.

In 2013, Joanne became the president of the entire MSF organisation. She led a team of over 35,000 people across the globe, caring for whoever needed their help.

And it all started when she picked up that book.

Of course, Joanne might not be the type of hero we see in films, but if leading an organisation that helps people in danger isn't heroic, then I'm not really sure what is.

Like me, Joanne found her dream between the covers of a book. But that's not the only place we can look for dreams. We can find them anywhere, which makes it important to look out for things that inspire us. Whenever I couldn't find something in my bedroom, my mum would say, 'It's not going to jump out and hit you in the face.' Unless I was looking for my sister, she was usually right. What also became clear was that the things I was looking for were never in the places I expected them to be. If they were, it wouldn't be so hard to find them.

Socks aren't hard to find when they're in the sock drawer. They're hard to find when they're in the fridge or the biscuit jar or the sweet tin that doesn't have sweets in it anymore, just old batteries and sticky coins.

DREAMS TOO
can often be found
IN THE PLACES
WHERE PEOPLE
least expect
TO FIND THEM.

They can leap out of books or films or songs or games you play with friends. They can arrive fully formed or they can grow slowly inside us, as we learn more and more about certain topics, places, people or events.

One friend of mine was ten years old when he went to the British Museum on a school trip and stumbled into the exhibit on Egyptians. He was instantly hooked. He's now an Egyptologist who spends a lot of time pottering around ancient tombs and trying to decipher messages that are over two thousand years old.

Another friend of mine was taken to the circus every year as a child but didn't take up juggling until he was thirty, after years spent being an accountant. Juggling was a dream that had been inside him since childhood, it just needed a little time to come out. And now he performs at festivals and fairs all over England. No one has to decide exactly what they want to do with their life while they're young.

YOU ALSO DON'T HAVE TO EVER SETTLE ON JUST ONE DREAM.

Dreams can grow and change, as we do.

Take the case of Ellen MacArthur, who found herself reading an entirely different kind of book to Joanne or me. Ellen's book was an adventure story called *Swallows and Amazons*.

Ellen was so captivated by this book she started saving up for her own boat.

For three years, she skipped school meals[1] and saved enough money to buy her first little vessel.

Ten years later, Ellen sailed alone around the world on a wildly dangerous journey.

[1] I'm not encouraging you to spend your lunch money on boats. You're probably human, so you definitely need food. If you want to raise money for a project you care about, try asking your parents for extra chores or looking for small bits of work like washing cars or delivering papers.

At certain points, the nearest humans to Ellen were the astronauts on the International Space Station somewhere up above her. She was utterly alone through the raging storms.

Ellen went on many more voyages and saw things that made her realise how vital it is to look after our planet.

If we don't stop polluting the earth, we'll all be in deep trouble.

Now retired from professional sailing, Ellen has created a foundation that aims to help the planet by reusing, recycling and re-purposing materials. She has also founded a trust that rebuilds the confidence of sick children by teaching them how to sail.

From a young age, Ellen had big dreams and goals. Once she'd achieved them, she found she had developed new dreams that involved using everything she'd learned to try and help others. 'How could sailing improve the lives of young people?' she wondered. And how could she look after the beautiful planet she'd spent years sailing across?

For me, that's what makes Ellen a hero. She sailed around the world, realised just how much the planet needed her help and decided to do something about it. She achieved her dream and found a new one along the way.

And just like Joanne, it all started when she picked up a book.

While learning about their two stories, I started to wonder what might have happened if neither Joanne nor Ellen had picked up those certain books. Would their lives have taken different paths? Or were they always destined to find their way to their passions?

I think they would have both found their dreams eventually, because both Ellen and Joanne had one very important thing in common: curiosity. There was a reason they'd opened those books; they wanted to know more. However they arrive, whether it's through novels or museums or circuses, our dreams come from paying attention to the world. They come from being curious. They drift in through open eyes and ears, like seeds looking for places to grow.

THREP'NY BIT

SO WHAT WAS THE LAST THING THAT MADE THE HAIRS ON THE BACK OF YOUR NECK STAND UP?

OR THE LAST THING TO KEEP YOU AWAKE AT NIGHT WITH EXCITEMENT?

WHAT IN THE WORLD ARE YOU MOST CURIOUS ABOUT?

Was there a book or a film or a lesson in school that inspired you?

WHAT IS THE MOST EXCITING JOB YOU CAN IMAGINE?

WHAT FASCINATES YOU?

Often, you have to go looking for dreams. They're more like socks than little sisters; they aren't always going to jump out and hit you in the face.

If you are lucky enough to find them, they can be difficult to hold on to. If they're too big, they can feel unachievable. If they're too small, they can feel unimportant. Almost everyone feels this way but a hero is someone who finds a way of pushing forward through the doubt and making their dream their superpower. It's very easy to feel intimidated by the world. To feel as though other people are more impressive or important. Or to feel like you're too small to make a difference.

I often feel like this too. When I do, I like to think about a man called Carl Sagan. Carl was a cosmologist, which means he studied the universe and everything in it. He was interested in stars and planets and space and time and all of those vast and mind-blowing topics that it feels like no-one will ever really understand.

On Valentine's Day in 1990, the spaceship known as Voyager 1 was about to leave our solar system. It would lose contact with the earthlings who made it and continue on in an endless, lonely journey through the cosmos. Just as it was about to leave the solar system, Carl Sagan asked the scientists in charge of the spacecraft if they could turn its cameras around and take one last picture of Earth.

'But Carl,' they protested. 'What scientific data will that give us?'

'None at all,' he said. 'But please do it anyway.'

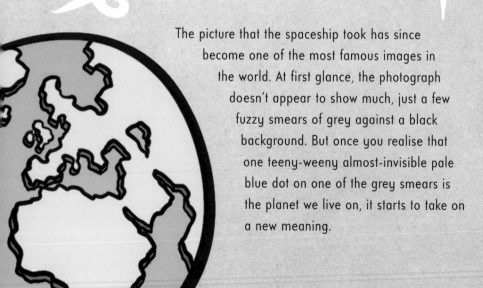

The picture that the spaceship took has since become one of the most famous images in the world. At first glance, the photograph doesn't appear to show much, just a few fuzzy smears of grey against a black background. But once you realise that one teeny-weeny almost-invisible pale blue dot on one of the grey smears is the planet we live on, it starts to take on a new meaning.

For Carl, the picture taught him that it was up to us **'to deal more kindly with one another and to preserve and cherish the pale blue dot, the only home we've ever known.' For me, the picture serves as a reminder of what really matters.**

You might be small, compared to the universe, but so is everyone else. We are all tiny dots on a tiny dot and, no matter how big or small our dreams may seem, we are no more or less important than each other.

I should be honest with you here: I have not yet made it to Antarctica. That doesn't mean I've let go of the dream or that I don't still carry it with me, but it has reared its head in other ways. I have written stories featuring polar explorers, I still read books about doomed expeditions and I am always looking for ways that I can talk my way onto a ship bound for the South Pole.

If you're someone like Joanne, your dreams might stay the same from the moment they arrive in your brain until the day your hair turns grey. If you're someone like me or Ellen, however, your dreams might change shape as you grow. You might find other things you care about or are good at or decide are important.

Tomorrow, I might decide to never write another word again, and instead learn how to make furniture. (In which case the rest of this book will be blank and I suggest you use it for playing noughts and crosses or drawing self-portraits.) Or I might go back to school, learn what the inside of a horse looks like and start training as a vet. And next week, maybe you'll have a funny French lesson that inspires you to move to Paris, and train at clown school.[1]

---

[1] There are a few different clown schools in France. Perhaps the most famous is run by Philippe Gaulier, who some actors have called the funniest man alive.

It doesn't matter if you have one dream, or five or a hundred. It doesn't matter if your dream stays the same from when you're five until you're ninety-five, or whether you're constantly discovering new ones. What matters is that your dreams mean something to you.

I WILL WRITE STORIES ABOUT EXPLORERS IN ANTARCTICA.

I will sail alone around the world.

I WILL HELP THOSE WHO NEED IT MOST.

TRY MAKING A LIST OF YOUR DREAMS.

They might be dreams you've had for a long time or they might be dreams that have just floated into your head. They can be as wild, as scary, as big, as small, as distant or as close as you want. You could have a dream for tomorrow and a dream for ten or twenty or fifty years from now. You could have a dream that involves your best friend and another that involves the entire population of your town. Whenever something new comes into your head, add it to the list.

Watch your list grow. Watch which dreams stay with you and which ones fade, to be replaced by other dreams.

At first, the list might just be a list, but everything that any human has ever done started life as an idea in their head. Lightbulbs, ham sandwiches and trainers that light up were all ideas before they became reality. So were the first spaceships to land on the moon. Every doctor that has ever saved a life had the idea to become a doctor first. While every founder of a charity would've thought about how they could make a difference before they actually did it. All heroes share a common dream: to make the world a better place. And there are thousands of different ways of going about it.

What is important is that you let your imagination run free. Seek out the things that excite you and come up with grand plans of how to get involved with them. Don't worry about what other people have done and don't worry about what anyone thinks of the things that you want to do. Every hero started out with a dream. Every one of them was once where you are now.

And like every hero that has ever existed, you're here, spending your time on the pale blue dot. It is up to you what to do with it.

2

> 'TO BE YOURSELF IN A WORLD
> THAT IS CONSTANTLY TRYING TO
> MAKE YOU SOMETHING ELSE IS THE
> GREATEST ACCOMPLISHMENT.'
> – Ralph Waldo Emerson

It is very hard to become good at something you don't like doing. Actually, it's hard to get good at anything, but getting good at something you don't enjoy is like trying to catch a pigeon with your bare hands.

WHY?

Well, if you like doing something – say, making puppets or eating hotdogs, for example – then you're likely to spend a lot of time doing it. And the more time you spend doing it, the better you get. There are exceptions, of course. Maybe your parents force you to play the clarinet every single night until your tongue feels like it's going to fall off. You'll get better, but you might end up wanting to smash your clarinet to pieces. (Then again, maybe you'll hate the clarinet at first but, over time, you'll learn to love it. This is exactly what happened with me and mayonnaise.)

Mostly though, we spend more time on the things we enjoy and those are the things we get better at. That's why, when I was in school, I became much better at guitar than maths, got higher scores on PlayStation games than in physics, and knew more about polar explorers than I did about Tudor kings.

We're lucky that things turn out that way. It means that we all end up developing our own particular set of interests and talents. It means I have friends who paint huge oil paintings and others who work on the maths behind how best to deliver pizza (yes, that's a real job[1]). It means some people in the world know a lot about Henry VIII and other people know a lot about those little red bugs that smell like farts if you accidently squash them.[2]

We all have DIFFERENT SKILLS AND INTERESTS. We pursue them and we grow into different people.

The problem is that it might sometimes feel like the skill or passion you have isn't as important or interesting as the things other people like. Imagine that you're at a school where everybody is obsessed with football. All everybody talks about is football, all everybody watches is football and all everybody plays in every spare moment of the day is football. What if you don't like football? What if you like juggling or playing the flute or reading books about polar explorers?

[1] To make sure every pizza is delivered hot, someone's job is to write computer codes to work out how best to schedule the deliveries!
[2] Sometimes called 'stink bugs' or 'shield bugs'. They're harmless to us but they can totally ruin crops.

You want to fit in, of course. You want to be able to talk to everyone else and share jokes, but it can be difficult to do this if you're not particularly interested in the things other people are interested in.

Here is something I didn't find out until I left school: while you're at school, most people don't want to be different. You want to fit in. You want to be the same as everyone else. But once school is over, you will find that it's your differences that make you an asset to the world. It's your differences that make you exciting. It's your differences that mean you can make a difference.

Think about everyone you've ever been amazed or inspired by. Were they the same as everyone else? Or did they stand out? Was there something that set them apart from other people?

There's a place for every talent and passion. Even if there aren't people at school who share your interest, there will be people throughout the world who do. And there will be places where you can put it to great use. It may not be on a football pitch, it may not make you rich enough to buy a jet-ski, but so many skills, interests and passions can be used to make the world a brighter place, both for you and for other people. Whether it's through raising money for charity, helping those who need your help, or simply spreading joy, everything has the potential to become a superpower. A superpower, after all, is any power that is used to help others.

Sakdiyah Ma'ruf is a comedian from Java, Indonesia. For Sakdiyah, the passion she discovered when she was young was American comedy. She would spend hours in front of the TV watching funny American shows. Growing up in Indonesia, this was how Sakdiyah taught herself English.

One day, Sakdiyah was watching a comedian called Robin Williams.

His performance showed Sakdiyah that comedians could talk about serious issues while making jokes at the same time.

Laughter can be a powerful force for good!

Sakdiyah decided to use comedy to confront an issue that was close to her heart: the unfair way women were being treated in her culture.

She began with a comedy performance at her school's talent competition. She came second and at that moment had found what she wanted to do.

Ever since then, Sakdiyah has performed comedy that makes people cry with laughter while also shining a light on serious issues. Sakdiyah uses her comedy to fight for positive change.

Sakdiyah found that her passion was comedy, discovered she could make people laugh, and realised that by developing this skill she could use it to fight for the kind of world she wanted to live in.

SOMETIMES IT ISN'T WHAT YOU DO, BUT THE WAY YOU DO IT THAT CAN HAVE THE BIGGEST EFFECT ON THE WORLD.

I used to spend most half-term holidays lying in my bed eating chocolate chips and playing games on my phone. When my mum noticed that I was spending days doing absolutely nothing, she sent me to a local village hall where a man who'd once worked in a circus taught kids how to ride unicycles, juggle and spin plates over the holidays.

This was not my idea of fun. In fact, it was my idea of whatever the opposite of fun is. I tried desperately to convince my mum that I ought to be left at home, eating chocolate chips and watching episodes of TV shows I'd already seen six times before. She wouldn't listen.

But it quickly turned out to be far more enjoyable than I'd thought. By the end of that half-term, rather than having eaten nineteen bags of chocolate chips, I'd made friends, learned how to ride a unicycle and worked together with people to create an extraordinary show. I ended the holiday excited and energised, rather than lazy and lonely.

The man who ran that camp became a hero to me, and not just because he could breathe fire, but because he'd given me something to get excited about.

A hero isn't just someone who steps in when they see things going wrong. A hero can be someone who spreads joy too, a person who focuses on brightening up people's lives or bringing people together.

And almost any talent can be used to bring people together. Whether it's doing circus skills, playing football or trying to figure out how to reach the moon, most people enjoy working with others. It's what we evolved to do, all the way back from when our prehistoric ancestors had to head out in groups and hunt for their dinner. Working together gives us a purpose and helps us flourish.

When we work together, there can be amazing and unexpected results. Take the example of this group of artists from Mexico.

Las Palmitas is a neighbourhood in the town of Pachuca, Mexico. For many years, its citizens felt unsafe because of the high crime rates.

One day, the government decided to call in the German Crew, a group of young graffiti artists who used their art as a way of uniting communities.

Working together with the locals, the artists painted over two hundred houses in bright and wonderful colours. They turned Las Palmitas into a beautiful, colourful, joyful piece of art. Enrique Gomez, the project director, noticed a real difference after the painting was finished.

People are really changing. They are growing, there is more community spirit.

Since the German crew worked with the residents of Las Palmitas, crime has reduced by 79 per cent. The people who live there are happier and feel safer.

The German Crew brought people together to work on one big project and managed to reduce crime with the help of their art. Sounds pretty heroic to me!

Most of us imagine superheroes as people who stop crime by fighting evil villains, but as the German Crew proved: there is more than one way of going about things.

Running circus skills camps or creating paintings may not look quite as impressive as swooping down from a great height to save someone's life, but it has the same effect:

MAKING THE PLACE WE LIVE HAPPIER AND SAFER.

Both the German Crew and the man who ran the circus skills camp made a difference by bringing people together. But, a superpower that unites people and gives them joy and hope can come in many forms.

For years, Dino Impagliazzo worked as a chef in Italy, until the day came for him to retire. One day, Dino was walking through a train station in Rome when he got talking to a man who was homeless.

There's never anywhere I can get food on Sundays.

Dino realised he had exactly the kind of skill that could help. That Sunday, he made food and gave it out to the people living on the streets around the train station.

Soon after that, Dino started bringing together volunteers to cook huge meals that could feed even bigger numbers of hungry people.

At the age of 90, Dino is now known as the 'chef of the poor'. Together with his group of volunteers, he manages to serve over 32,000 meals every year.

Dino realised he had a superpower that could be used for good and he didn't let it go to waste.

You might find you love comedy and choose to use it to fight for what you believe in. You might find you love art and choose to use it to bring joy to your neighbours. And you might find you love cooking and choose to use your skills to feed others. What makes a skill a superpower is not necessarily the skill itself, but the way in which it is used. Applying make-up is a superpower if you use it to give people confidence. Football is a superpower if you use the fame it gives you to raise awareness about important issues. And comedy is a superpower if you can use it to fight for change.

Something that might surprise you is how your interests and talents can end up fitting together. Things that you never thought would be of any use to the world can also find a way of proving useful. Really useful. And in totally unexpected ways.

For one Dutch man, Bart Weetjens, it was his love of rats that turned out to shape his life. As a child, Bart kept rats. When he grew older, Bart wanted to dedicate his life to helping people. In particular, he wanted to help people in African countries where landmines had been left behind after wars. These dangerous devices lie hidden in the ground and explode if someone steps on them. They are VERY dangerous. Bart wondered whether the rats he'd kept as a child would be capable of stepping onto landmines without setting them off. If they could, might the rats be able to detect the devices and save lives in the process? It turned out he was right. Bart ended up creating a charity that trained rats to find landmines, so that they could be safely removed before they hurt anyone. He has now saved thousands of innocent lives.

It was exactly **BECAUSE** he had the unusual passion for rats that Bart was able to come up with an idea no-one else would have done.

Can you imagine if Bart had given up on rats while he was in school? I doubt it made him very popular and there probably weren't a lot of other kids who he could chat about rats with. But Bart's unusual passion turned out to be something that huge numbers of people now owe their lives to. I've never saved anyone's life. Or at least not knowingly. But I have found that my strengths and interests have become parts of my life in ways I would have never predicted. Reading about polar explorers gave me a passion for books, and is exactly why I'm writing this to you now. Some of the books I've written have been enjoyed by people. A few have even said they made them feel a little less alone or afraid. It might be a small thing, but it's what I'm able to do.

In the last chapter I told you to make a list of your dreams, but now I want you to think about the things that you're already good at. It can be absolutely anything: Origami? Singing? Baking? Listening? Telling stories?

Now I want you to think about how this talent could be used to make the world a better place. You don't have to try and work out how to save lives with your saxophone, but try to come up with a way that your talent might benefit others. It could involve raising money, helping others or just brightening up your friends' days. Every talent can be a superpower. Every interest can lead you somewhere exciting. If you pursue the things you care about, rather than the things other people think are important, you'll never end up trying to catch a pigeon with your bare hands.

3

> 'THE PURPOSE OF LIFE IS TO
> DISCOVER YOUR GIFT. THE MEANING
> OF LIFE IS TO GIVE YOUR GIFT AWAY.'
> – David Viscott

There will always be someone who needs your help. In fact, there will always be lots of people who need your help, and some of them might be standing next to you right now, while others are oceans away. Some might be more vulnerable than you, or less privileged, or they might just be a friend having a bad day who needs cheering up. People need help with everything, from pulling splinters out their fingers to getting enough food to eat.

It takes a hero to realise when someone needs your help and to figure out the best way of giving it to them.

For six-year-old Ryan Hreljac, the day that he decided to help people would change his life forever. And it started just like any other day. He put on his socks, as normal. Ate his cereal, as normal. And walked to school, as normal. (If I'm honest, I don't know if Ryan did eat cereal or walk to school. Or wear socks, for that matter. But I do know a bit about what happened after that.)

At school, Ryan and his class were taught about how difficult it is for certain people in parts of Africa to get clean water.

Many have to travel huge distances each day. Often the water is so dirty that it makes them sick and can even lead to death.

What if there's a way that I can help?

Ryan did some research and discovered that the price of building a well in Uganda was around $2000. For four months, he earned pocket money by doing as many chores around the house as possible and saved all the money he could.

It wasn't enough.

He started raising funds by talking about his project wherever he could and asking more people for donations. Eventually, with a huge amount of hard work, Ryan managed to raise $2000. It meant that a village in Uganda were given a well that could provide them with clean water for years to come. Not long after, he created a charity called Ryan's Well Foundation and got to work changing the world.

More than twenty years later, Ryan is still in charge of Ryan's Well Foundation. The charity have provided almost one million people with access to clean water and have worked in over one thousand communities in seventeen countries.

'The world is like a great big puzzle and we all have to figure out where our puzzle piece fits. I figure my piece fits with clean water. I just hope everyone else finds out where their puzzle piece fits too.'

– Ryan Hreljac

But you don't need to look to other countries to find people in need.

There's probably someone in your house who needs help. Maybe one of your parents needs help peeling carrots.

There's probably someone in your class at school who needs help. Maybe they're struggling to make friends or need help understanding what happened to all of Henry VIII's wives.

There could be people in your town who need help. They might be trying to clear a park of litter or paint over graffiti.

There are people all over your country who definitely need help, with everything from doing their shopping to learning to read to walking their dog or clearing the leaves out of their garden. But there are also people across the world who need help.

EVEN OUR PLANET, AS YOU PROBABLY KNOW, IS STARTING TO NEED OUR HELP.

It can feel overwhelming, thinking of how many people in the world need help. In fact, it can feel so overwhelming that it's difficult to know where to start. I know I sometimes feel scared by the idea.

Have you ever seen those charity adverts on TV? Ones that talk about an animal that has been treated badly or a person living in poverty?

Researchers discovered that if people see the story of one person suffering, they're more likely to help than if they hear that millions of people are suffering. This isn't because people don't care, it's because when you see an individual story, you probably think that you could make a difference to that person. But when you hear that millions of people are suffering, you probably think that it's such a huge problem there's no way you could make a difference, so there's no point trying.

But there's *always* a point in trying. Ryan proved that. He may have started off with one small concrete goal – to give one well to one village – but once he'd achieved this, his dreams grew. After he'd managed to help a few people, Ryan realised the difference he was capable of making in the lives of others, and he became determined to do even more.

When you try, you have a chance to make a difference, not just in the lives of others but in your own life too.

Much happier, in fact, than the things we normally think will make us happy. I sometimes think I'll be happy if I buy certain clothes (I'm not supposed to tell you the brand names in case it looks like I was paid to advertise them). If I really pay attention, though, I can see that spending money on clothes that I don't need makes me far less happy than spending money on useful things for other people. Doing things for others makes me happier than doing things for myself. And it's probably true for you too.

I'll try and prove it to you.

Well, scientists have found that those things are unlikely to make you as happy as you expect. Me and you, as human beings, are very bad at guessing which things will make us happy.

Part of the reason is that once you own something like a big house, you get used to it. You get used to everything. You'd get used to a green sky or having hands made of broccoli if you had to.

It makes me think of a school trip I once went on to a sewage works. As you might have guessed, no-one was particularly thrilled about this trip. The school across town had gone on a trip to France. My cousin's school had gone to a theme park. And we got to go and look at big tanks of poo.

As soon as we stepped off the bus, everyone started gagging at the smell and screaming that they were going to be sick. It only took us about half an hour to get used to the smell of being surrounded by poo. After that, no-one noticed it again. And if we could all get used to that smell, then you could definitely get used to a house with a cinema and a swimming pool.

Okay, you might be thinking, maybe big houses don't make us happy and school trips to the sewage works aren't that bad, but why would that mean helping people is going to make me happier?

A scientist named Sonja Lyubomirsky from the University of California has done a lot of research in this area. In her studies, Sonja would split students into groups. Some she would tell to do nothing over the following weeks, and others she would tell to start doing kind things for other people. She didn't specify what sort of kind things. It could have been absolutely anything. The students who performed kind acts reported being happier themselves, not just immediately afterwards, but for up to one month after they'd done nice things for people. What Sonja also found was that the more different types of kind acts they performed, the bigger the effect on their own happiness.

And you're never too young or too old to start. Someone who found an unusual way of helping others is 100-year-old Captain Tom Moore. During his life, he fought in the Second World War, raced motorbikes, survived skin cancer and had two children. When coronavirus started spreading throughout the UK, Captain Tom decided he would do his part in the fight against it.

The heroic hospital staff were putting themselves at risk of catching the disease as they tried to save lives. Captain Tom wanted to do his bit to help the British doctors and nurses. In the lead-up to his 100th birthday, he began walking laps of his garden to raise money for a charity supporting the NHS.

First, Tom aimed to raise £1000. When he reached that goal, he upped his target to £5000. He was amazed by the response he was getting. Soon, Captain Tom was appearing on TV channels across the world. The donations came flooding in. He eventually raised over thirty million pounds for people working in British hospitals.

Captain Tom even released a number one charity single, becoming the oldest person ever to top the UK charts!

Captain Tom showed the world how everybody is capable of doing something to help people in need. If someone who has been alive since before TV was invented can find a way of doing their part, then most of us probably can, too. And we should, because there will be many times in your life when you need to ask other people for help. If your parents are anything like mine were, they probably say to you:

TREAT OTHERS AS YOU WANT TO BE TREATED YOURSELF.[1]

This is known as the Golden Rule.

It has existed across many cultures of the world for a lot longer than my parents have. Our first recorded example of the Golden Rule comes from China, over two and a half thousand years ago. **The philosopher Confucius said, 'What you do not wish for yourself, do not do to others.'** This may be the first written example but the ancient Egyptians came up with the same idea, as did some African religions, Indian religions, Abrahamic religions and the civilisations of Greece, Rome and Persia. So there must be something in it.

[1] (Or, 'If you flick your sister, then I'm going to flick you harder.')

IN SEVERAL CULTURES, THE GOLDEN RULE HAS BEEN TOLD THROUGH A STORY ABOUT VERY LONG SPOONS.

There are many versions of the story but they generally involve people trying to eat food with, as you might have guessed, very long spoons.

The people who try to feed themselves with the very long spoons end up getting no food in their mouths and probably quite a lot on their clothes. But the people who choose to feed each other with the very long spoons end up feeling happy and full.

I'm not sure how often you will find yourself trying to eat with very long spoons, but the principle remains the same: we'll all do better if we help each other rather than only trying to help ourselves.
Take Penny Brown, for instance, a nurse from New York.

One day, Penny was watching her son play baseball when a bat hit another player named Kevin in the chest.

Kevin's heart stopped.

Penny rushed to help him. She knew CPR and was able to save his life.

Seven years later, Penny was eating in a restaurant.

Suddenly, a piece of food got stuck in her throat. She started to choke. Desperately, Penny tried to ask for help.

Luckily, a young man who worked in the restaurant was a member of the volunteer fire brigade and knew what to do. He ran to Penny's aid and gave her the Heimlich manoeuvre, clearing her airways and allowing her to breathe again.

It turned out the young man was Kevin. The boy who Penny saved all those years before had ended up saving her life in return.

It's clear that helping people doesn't only benefit the person in need. You don't have to take my word for it. Try acting out one of Sonja's experiments for yourself. First, spend a week not changing your behaviour, but noting down how you feel. It's probably easiest to do this at the end of the day, perhaps when you have a spare second before you go to bed. You only have to put down a couple of words. Here, mine would look like this:

MONDAY:
Boring. Couldn't concentrate. Didn't get anything done. 4/10.

TUESDAY:
Got pooed on by a bird. 3/10.

WEDNESDAY:
Ate too many crisps and didn't get enough sleep. Everyone was annoying. 5/10.

And so on. Then, in the following week, set yourself the task of doing one kind thing to help another person each day. It can be as big or as small as you want. Try to vary the kinds of things you help with, from giving a friend some tips on his homework, to helping make dinner, signing a petition or donating a few pence to charity. Just make sure that at the end of the day, you jot down a couple of words about how this made you feel. When the two weeks are up, compare your notes about how you were feeling over those days.

If helping others is making you happier, then why not continue? (If it's not making you happier, you can write a letter of complaint to my publisher. But I think you'll be surprised.)

By being a hero and helping other people, you'll end up helping yourself.

You'll make friends.
You'll feel happier.
And, if you ever find yourself struggling to eat soup with an incredibly long spoon, you'll know exactly what to do.

NO ACT OF KINDNESS IS TOO SMALL

4

'THE MIRACLE IS THIS – THE MORE WE SHARE, THE MORE WE HAVE.'
– Leonard Nimoy

At the moment, I spend quite a lot of time in a small village in the north of Bulgaria. It's very peaceful. Tall, ancient cliffs stand guard around the houses. A muddy river curls through the valley. Most of the people who used to live there have left, leaving the houses empty and large numbers of animals without homes. Among my neighbours are an elderly couple named Ivan and Penka who have lived in the village for the majority of their lives. Together, they feed over fifty cats every day. Though they do not have a lot of money, each day they make sure every one of the cats that turns up in their garden has something to eat. For those cats, Ivan and Penka are everything. Without their help, they'd be lost and hungry.

Acts like giving food or offering shelter might seem like small things to us but they can turn out to mean the world to other people (or cats). You never know what effect the kindness you show someone might have on their day. You never know how badly someone might need that smile you flash them as they pass you in the corridor or those crisps you share with them at lunch.

Te Paea Hinerangi was from New Zealand. She was Māori, one of the indigenous people of her country, and she worked as a tour guide around Lake Rotomahana in the 1870s. Many people spoke about Te Paea Hinerangi's kindness and intelligence.

In 1886, while taking a group of tourists across the lake, Te Paea saw a waka wairua.[1]

Eleven days later, a nearby volcano violently erupted. It threw ash, mud and rock into the air. Dangerous electric storms swirled through the sky.

[1] This was a phantom canoe filled with spirits. It had a crew of 13, all with the heads of dogs! She saw it as a warning of grave danger.

Te Paea opened the doors of her home and allowed in anyone who needed shelter. As debris rained from the sky,

they huddled together in her home.

Many people died during the eruption, but Te Paea's house managed to withstand the weight of falling debris. Because she had opened the doors of her house, Te Paea saved the lives of sixty people. Had she kept her door closed, they may well not have made it.

Te Paea went on to encourage lots of other Māori women to become guides around their beautiful country. She travelled around telling the story of how she had survived the terrifying eruption and continuing to lead bands of tourists through the spectacular nature of New Zealand. She's still remembered today for her act of kindness.

Allowing people to shelter in your house during a storm might seem like a small thing. Of course she did that, you might think, that's not heroic, I'd do that too.

But when scary things happen, it's often easier to think something along the lines of 'I'm sure those people out there will be fine.' Or, 'I'm sure they have their own houses to shelter in.' Or, 'I'm sure someone else will invite them in.'

Psychologists call that last one 'the bystander effect'. It just means that if you can see other people around when someone needs help, you're less likely to help them because you assume someone else will do it. And the more people you can see around you, the less likely you are to help.

Heroes, however, are not bystanders. Heroes are heroes because, unless the situation is too dangerous or there's nothing they can do, they are the ones who step in and offer their help.

It takes a hero to accept responsibility, even when there are others around them.

Because if everyone assumes someone else is going to help, then there will be no-one who actually does.

As well as directly helping people, our small acts of kindness can also end up encouraging others to do similar things.

Rhett Diessner, a professor of psychology at Lewis-Clarke State College, has found that certain areas of our brains light up when we see people doing acts of kindness. This makes us feel positive emotions and can lead to us copying the behaviours we've seen.

So if someone sees you doing something kind, however small, it might make them more likely to go out and be kind, too. After all, isn't that how we learn to do anything – by watching other people do it? I'd never dipped chips in a milkshake until I saw a friend do it. Once I saw it, I started doing it too. And once my sister saw me doing it, she quickly got onboard.

This idea was used as the plot of a film called *Pay It Forward*. If you're ever bored on a rainy day, you might want to have a look and see if you can find it.

 The film follows a twelve-year-old boy called Trevor, who is given a school assignment of finding a small way to make the world a better place. Trevor comes up with an idea called 'pay it forward'. The idea involves him doing three kind things for other people, and then asking each of them to also do kind things for three other people, and asking each of them to do kind things for three more people, and so on.

Over the course of the film, lots of different people end up doing lots of kind things for each other. It's a nice idea, right? And, if Rhett's research is right, you might not even have to tell people to pay it forward, they'll want to do it anyway.

Sometimes, when you're feeling down, all it takes is someone telling you that you're great, to brighten up your day. Imagine that I told three people that I thought they were great, and the next day each of those three people told three other people they thought they were great, and this continued, how many days do you think it would take before everyone in the world had been told they were great? I'll be honest, I couldn't work it out. So I asked a friend who's a mathematician. He said the calculation involved something called a geometric series and that the answer is:

if three people
told
THREE NEW PEOPLE
each day,

→

it would only take
around
21
DAYS

→

for every person
in the world
to have been told
THEY WERE GREAT.

It's amazing, isn't it, to think how such big effects might spring from small actions? What this proves is that to be a hero and make a big difference, you don't necessarily have to do something huge. **A hero can be someone who does something very small.** In fact, it seems to me like there may be many heroes among us who are doing very small things all the time, we just don't hear about them that often.

Rather than trying to get famous or be well-liked, they are helping others because it's what they feel is right. And the more of us who can follow their example, the bigger the effects will be.

Trevor, the boy in *Pay It Forward*, was not a hero because he did something huge, but because from his small actions, there were big effects. Inspired by the film, there's now even a 'Pay It Forward Day', on April 28th, when people from over 80 countries pledge to perform acts of kindness for strangers.

Why not try starting your own chain reaction

It might be easier than you think. You don't necessarily have to tell people to do things for others, but you could find a way of helping that frees them up to help others too. For example, you could tell your dad you'll take over the washing up, so that he can go and help your sister with her homework. Actions like that might end up having bigger effects than you can imagine.

Rhett's research, for example, also showed that a person doesn't even have to perform acts of kindness themselves to become happier, it's enough to see others doing them. So, if you see people doing kind things, it'll make you feel like you live in a kinder, safer world, and it'll make you happier to be where you are. It's much better than seeing people do unkind things. How would that make you feel about the people you were sharing a planet with? Kind acts, no matter how small, can brighten up the days of so many people. Like stones being dropped into still water, they can have effects that ripple outwards in huge circles.

Choi Dae Ho is a martial artist from South Korea. One summer, he travelled to Singapore with his martial arts team to compete in a Taekwando competition.

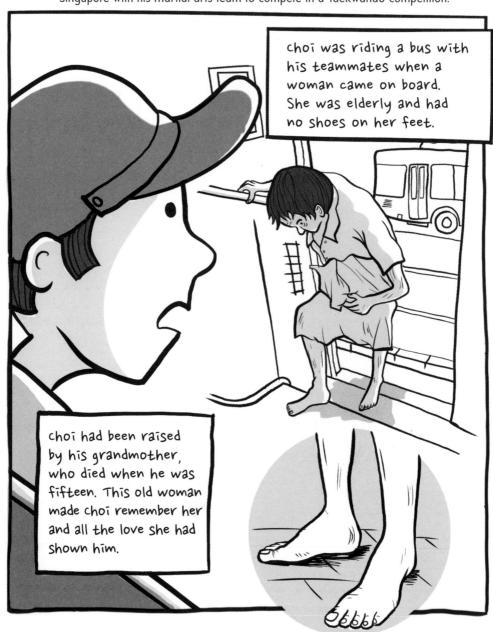

Choi was riding a bus with his teammates when a woman came on board. She was elderly and had no shoes on her feet.

Choi had been raised by his grandmother, who died when he was fifteen. This old woman made Choi remember her and all the love she had shown him.

He walked to where she was sitting, took off his shoes, and put them onto the old woman's feet. She looked at him and smiled. He went back to his seat.

When he got off the bus, Choi had to walk barefoot across the scorching hot pavement back to his hostel. Later, thanks to a photo someone secretly took of Choi and the smiling woman, his act of kindness became known across the world.

People loved hearing the story of the young martial artist from Korea helping an elderly woman he didn't know in a country he'd never been to before.

Choi said he couldn't understand why everyone made such a big fuss.
He was no hero. To him, it was just a little act of kindness, inspired by
the love that his grandmother had shown him when he was growing up.

But every act of kindness has an impact on the world. Sometimes
an act of kindness will have effects beyond what you can imagine.
Sometimes it can inspire others to do the same. And other times it can
just let people know that the world is the kind of place they can feel
safe in.

**Kindness is about more than giving away
your shoes or opening the door of your house.
Kindness is about acknowledging the fact
that we are all in this together.**

**We are all sharing a little wet planet in a
strange solar system in the Milky Way, and
it's a much nicer place to be when
we look out for each other.**

**That's why a hero knows that
no act of kindness is too small.**

SOMETIMES,
THE TINIEST DISPLAY
OF KINDNESS CAN
MEAN AS MUCH TO
SOMEONE AS SAVING
THE ENTIRE WORLD.

DON'T COMPARE YOURSELF TO OTHERS

5

'BE YOURSELF, EVERYONE ELSE IS ALREADY TAKEN.'
- Anonymous

It can feel quite daunting to read about the lives of people who have done incredible things. As someone who's written about hundreds of amazing people, I often find myself thinking, how do I compare? How will I ever become so important or amazing or talented? What if I'm just an ordinary person? What if I'm never going to be a hero?

It took me some time to realise that I am an ordinary person and all those people I'd written about were, too. Remember Carl Sagan's picture of the pale blue dot? Maybe you're top of the class, maybe you're able to kick a football into the top corner of a goal or maybe you're someone who hasn't found their superpower yet. Nevertheless we are all still just a little dot on our little dot. No matter who they are or where they come from, most people in the world still worry about silly things, or hate certain foods or wake up in the night trembling because of a nightmare. And whether you're good at sports, music or art, there will always be someone who can run faster than you or beat you at chess or paint a more realistic-looking picture of a horse.

You might see this most clearly when you make the move from primary to secondary school. While at primary school you might be the best at chess or long jump or armpit-farts, when you suddenly find yourself in a school ten times the size, you might not be the best anymore. And that's okay.

We can't hang our happiness on being the best at things. Otherwise we'll always be disappointed. (Unless you're Usain Bolt. And if you are Usain Bolt, then hi, it's a pleasure to have you with us. My nan is a huge fan.) Even if you are the best at something for a brief period of time, eventually you won't be anymore. People get older. Records get broken. New, louder methods of armpit-farting are devised. Usain Bolt can't be the fastest runner in the world forever. Eventually, someone else will take his place.

If we keep comparing
ourselves to others,
we end up getting jealous.
We end up being mean.
We start forgetting to be happy
with the things we have.

One of the most helpful things I was ever told to do was start each morning by listing three things I'm grateful for. My first response to this suggestion was: there's no way I'm doing that, that sounds very boring and I don't see the point. Besides, mornings are for eating Weetabix and watching TV. But I did try it. And the more I tried it, the more I started to see the benefit of doing this.

Here are the three things I was grateful for this morning:

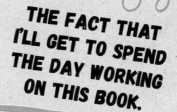

THE FACT THAT I'LL GET TO SPEND THE DAY WORKING ON THIS BOOK.

THE TREE OUTSIDE MY BEDROOM WINDOW, WHICH TURNS THE SUNLIGHT GREEN AND KEEPS THE NEIGHBOURS FROM KNOWING HOW MUCH TIME I SPEND IN BED.

THE PIZZA PLACE AROUND THE CORNER THAT I'M GOING TO ORDER FROM TONIGHT
(spicy pepperoni with red onions, if you're interested.)

Immediately, that sets me up for a day where I'm aware of the things I have, enjoy and care about. Who cares what anyone else has or does? These are the things I have and do. And I'm grateful for them.

TRY IT. For a week, find time to jot down the things you're grateful for. You'll find it easier to make a habit of if you do it at the same time each day; maybe first thing in the morning or last thing at night. At the start, you might think it's as pointless as I did. Eventually, you might begin to see the point.

When Chris Green, a runner from England, put aside the need to compare himself to others or be the best at what he did, he was able to make a huge difference.

Chris first saw rhinos on a trip to Kenya when he was ten years old.

Seeing them in their natural habitat sparked a passion for rhinos that would stay with Chris for his entire life.

When he discovered that rhinos are sometimes killed for their horns, he was determined to do something about it.

Today Chris has a day job in an office. But after work and at weekends, he trains for gruelling marathons and ultra-marathons,[1] which he runs to raise money for the animals he cares so much about.

He's often called 'Rhino boy' as he runs the races in a full rhino suit that weighs as much as a sausage dog!

[1] The ultra-marathons can be up to 100 miles long.

It doesn't matter that Chris isn't the best runner. It also doesn't matter that he probably won't win any of the races he's in (you try winning a race while wearing a rhino suit). What counts is that he runs for the rhinos. He uses the thing that he can do, to raise money for the creatures he cares so much about.

He's not going to break any records, but that isn't the point.

Chris is a hero because he doesn't compare himself to others, he runs for what he believes in.

And it helps. On the 25th anniversary of the Save the Rhino charity, Chris ran the London Marathon alongside 57 other rhino-lovers, and helped raise over £130,000.

The more we remember to keep an eye out for the things we have, the things we can do and the things we're grateful for, the easier it is to work out how we can make a difference.

WHAT ARE THE THINGS YOU'RE MOST GRATEFUL FOR?

WHAT ARE THE THINGS YOU CAN GIVE THE WORLD THAT NO-ONE ELSE CAN?

WHAT ARE THE THINGS YOU DO BECAUSE YOU TRULY ENJOY THEM?

HOW DO THEY FIT TOGETHER?

You might not be the best at guitar, but any song you write will be something that can only have come from you. You might not run the fastest, but maybe you're the only person who runs and also cares about a certain cause, in which case you might put the two together.

A young Canadian girl named Capri Everitt didn't set out to beat anyone either. Instead, she came up with something that no one had ever done before. In doing so, she connected with people and raised money for a cause she cared about. She became the best at her very own superpower.

One day Capri read a book called 'The World Needs Your Kid'. It inspired her to help children around the globe who had lost their parents or been abandoned.

Capri had grown up reading the 'Guinness Book of World Records' and she came up with a plan: she was going to break her very own record, and in the process she would raise money for the charity SOS Children's Villages.

Capri's goal was to break the record for the most national anthems sung in their host countries in one year.

She would travel the world, meet new people and learn how to sing the national anthem in the native language. Capri sang in 76 countries, learning the songs from locals, YouTube videos and diplomats.

From Italy to India, South Africa to Sweden, and the Czech Republic to China, Capri sang national anthems along with thousands of people around the world. In the process, she raised a lot of money for children who were less fortunate than she was.

It must have taken a great deal of courage to get up in front of so many different people and sing to them in their own language. If it was me, I would have been too afraid. I'm an awful singer compared to everyone else, I'd think. What if people laugh? Or boo?

But Capri did sing, and in those countries she made friends, formed bonds and learned about people and places she never would have known had she not decided to venture out across the globe.

Try coming up with your own record that needs **SETTING** rather than **BREAKING**. Something that **NO-ONE** has ever thought of doing before.

▶ MOST HANDSHAKES IN A MINUTE?

▶ BIGGEST MODEL GIRAFFE BUILT OUT OF PINECONES?

▶ LONGEST FOOT-BALL MATCH EVER PLAYED BETWEEN PEOPLE DRESSED AS CHARACTERS FROM HARRY POTTER?

How could you use a record like that to be a hero? Could it raise awareness for a cause? Bring the people of your community together? Or encourage people who are shy to get involved?

(Here's a tip: don't try anything food-related. I once tried to make a record for most crème eggs eaten in one minute. This left me feeling incredibly unwell for an unusually long time.)

OFTEN, IF WE COMPARE OURSELVES TO OTHERS, IT CAN STOP US DOING AMAZING THINGS.

I know it's held me back from doing things I've really wanted to do before, as I assume that someone else will always be able to do it better than I can. But if you stop comparing yourself to other people and try new things, you might be pleasantly surprised by the results.

When we're able to put an obsession with winning to one side and realise that there are more important things to aim for, then we become free to act in ways that will make us and the people around us happier. Remember what Sonja Lyubomirsky's studies showed? Doing things for others can make us happy. It's about making connections. It's about reaching out to other people, not trying to run faster than them. A hero doesn't compare themselves to other people, because they're too busy trying to help those other people out.

There may be moments when you have to make a choice between those two things. Do I focus on myself or do I put others first? It can be a hard decision to make. Take the example of Spanish athlete Ivan Fernandez Anaya.

Ivan was running behind Kenyan Olympic bronze-medallist Abel Mutai during a race in Navarre, Spain.

Ivan had been in second position for the entire race. At the final part of the race, Abel came to a stop and started cheering.

He thought he'd crossed the finish line.

 Actually, he hadn't.

Ivan came running up behind him. He could have easily sprinted past the other runner and won the race for himself. But he didn't.

Ivan stopped and tapped Abel on the shoulder, telling him he had to run further. He waited for Abel to cross the finishing line before he did.

Ivan's coach couldn't believe he had given up a chance of winning. But there's a reason Ivan is in this book and it's not because he was a pretty good runner. It's because he cared more about fairness than he did about beating someone else. Like a hero, he put kindness over his own gain. And I like to think he's happier now than he would have been if he'd zoomed past Abel Mutai when he had the chance.

If you keep comparing yourself to others, you'll never feel good enough.

There will always be ways in which other people are 'better' than you. Although this feeling can sometimes inspire you to work harder, comparing yourself too much can make you not want to bother trying in the first place.

Even people you wouldn't expect can feel like they're not good enough, just as often as you do. Even the richest people in the world and Olympic gold medallists and singers who've just had fifteen number one hits in a row. Why? Quite often, because they always want more than they have. It's worth remembering that however much you envy someone else, there are probably things about you that they envy. Even those singers with all the number ones probably wish that, like you, they could bake gooey cookies or play the trombone or walk through the streets without everyone staring at them.

This is where writing down the things we're grateful for comes in useful. It helps us to take stock of the things we do have, rather than dwelling on the things we don't.

Spiderman never sat around wondering whether his superpower was as cool as Superman's. And Batman certainly didn't sit around feeling sad that all the other superheroes had actual powers and all he had was a fast car and a tight suit. They all just got down to business trying to help whoever needed them. What good would comparing themselves to each other do? They'd only end up jealous and competitive. After all, you can rescue someone by swinging on spiderwebs, you can rescue someone by flying and you can rescue someone in a Batmobile. As long as you get me to safety, I wouldn't mind how you did it!

> An extraordinary person is just someone who does **EXTRAORDINARY THINGS.**

And being extraordinary doesn't mean being better than everyone else, it just means finding the things that make you ... well, you. We all have the capacity for being extraordinary. Maybe you can't shoot webs out your wrists or run faster than a greyhound, but that doesn't mean you can't help others. Chris, Capri and Ivan all proved that. They are heroes because they refused to get bogged down in the useless game of comparing themselves to others. Instead, they each chose to harness their unique superpowers to do something extraordinary.

DISCOVER EVERYTHING
YOU CAN

6

'LET US PICK UP OUR BOOKS AND OUR PENS, THEY ARE THE MOST POWERFUL WEAPONS.'
– Malala Yousafzai

Daisy Mora lived in the Rio Grande Valley, Colombia. Each day, she would travel to school on a zipline that went at 40 mph, while carrying her younger brother in a sack. It was incredibly dangerous but the only way to travel if they wanted to access education – something that many of us don't think twice about.

When I imagine that being my journey to school, I mostly think about the excuses I'd come up with for not going. (I don't like heights or ziplines and I tend to drop things, especially when I'm scared.) If I then heard about kids who could just walk twenty minutes to school, I'd grumble about how lucky they were.

I know it's hard to feel particularly lucky when you're made to haul yourself out of a warm bed at six o'clock on a January morning. And I also know that sometimes it can feel pointless when you're made to learn about things that don't seem to have any obvious use. When exactly will you need to know the names of Henry VIII's wives?

What use is physics, really? And why couldn't you just use the calculator on your phone if you ever need to add up the price of apples, pears and scarves?

But you might end up being surprised by just how useful certain bits of knowledge can be.

LEARNING is about so much more than making sure a few facts stay stuck inside your head. It's about **UNDERSTANDING THE BIG, STRANGE WORLD AROUND US.**

If a hero is going to change the world for the better, they'll have to understand it first. A hero has to know either the people they're trying to help, the situation they're trying to change or the causes they want to fight for. A hero has to have what might be one of the greatest superpowers: knowledge.[1] Without it, most other superpowers are useless.

---

[1] Possibly not as good as invisibility or the ability to turn into a giant green man, but very important nonetheless.

Someone who discovered how much of a superpower knowledge could be was Tilly Smith.

Tilly Smith was ten years old when she was on holiday in Phuket, Thailand.

While watching the sea, Tilly noticed that the water was pulling away from the shore and bubbles were forming over its surface.

It reminded her of a geography lesson she'd had in school. In that lesson, they'd learned about tsunamis, the dangerous waves that can occur after earthquakes.

Tilly went to tell her parents, who told hotel management. They rushed to evacuate everyone from the beach.

A few minutes later, a huge tsunami crashed into the shore. It was one of the many tsunamis that would cause so much devastation after the 2004 Indian Ocean Earthquake. Over two hundred thousand people died. But, thanks to Tilly, everyone who was on the beach that day survived.

Because of what she'd learned at school, Tilly heroically saved everyone on the beach.

What Tilly also managed to do was trust her instincts. She didn't doubt herself, even though she could well have thought: well, if there really is a tsunami coming, wouldn't someone else have noticed? Wouldn't the adults at the hotel be doing something about it?

In situations like this, it's often much better to be safe than sorry. What would have happened if Tilly had been wrong? Nothing, really. The hotel staff would have told her parents that it was okay, they didn't have to worry, the sea normally bubbled around that time of year. But Tilly refused to be a bystander. She took responsibility. She used her knowledge as a superpower that saved lives.

Tilly's story reminded me of an incredible act of heroism from a woman named Lizzie Wells.

Lizzie had survived skin cancer and wanted to be a brain surgeon, so she was training at medical school.

One day Lizzie was at home on her phone watching a TikTok video by a man called Alex Griswold.

Alex made funny videos and in one of them, he happened to show his back.

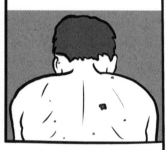

When Lizzie saw Alex's back in the video, she realised that one of his moles looked like it might be the beginning of a skin cancer.

She immediately sent Alex a message, suggesting he ought to go and see a doctor. Alex did get it checked out. The doctor told him that although it wasn't cancer yet, it would have become more dangerous if it had been left to grow unchecked. Alex quickly had an operation to get it removed. Lizzie may well have saved his life.

Lizzie and Tilly were both heroes because they managed to use their knowledge as a superpower. They both refused to be bystanders and insisted on trusting their instincts.

School may teach you some things, but others you can find out for yourself. Luckily, there are more ways than ever to do this. There are courses, clubs, books and other resources where you can learn about any topics that might interest you.

There are a huge number of online sites and programmes where you can learn all kinds of different things. Just last week I finished a free course on anthropology[1] and the week before that I did a course on the science of happiness.

Websites like The Khan Academy[2] host free lessons and courses on lots of subjects for all ages and abilities, in a number of different languages. A lot of the content consists of YouTube videos, that can make even the most complicated things seem easy to grasp. These can prove hugely useful, especially for things you want to learn about that haven't been covered in school, or things you might have touched on but would like to know more about.

Other websites that provide free learning include Coursera and edX, both of which offer free university-level courses in multiple languages, not just in the kinds of subjects you might study in school, but in things like first aid, survival skills, cracking codes, designing book covers, computer programming, money, meditation, digital music and a thousand other subjects. All you need to do is ask a parent, guardian or teacher to help you choose and enrol on a course, and you'll be ready to go.

[1] Anthropology is the study of humans, from our earliest ancestors to the people alive today.
[2] If you still have questions about the use of things you learn about in school, The Khan Academy have a great project for discussing that. It involves people who work at the animation studio Pixar, responsible for making films like *Finding Nemo*, *Toy Story*, and *The Incredibles*. In the project 'Pixar in

There is nothing to stop you
LEARNING ABOUT ANYTHING
you want to explore.

You have access to a world of knowledge at your fingertips. You could:

watch YouTube tutorials to learn a new language,

find out how to play the drums,

or even how to cook a lasagne.

I recently found that I was spending a lot of time flicking through social media comparing myself to other people, and I decided that I could use my time more wisely. I deleted the apps and downloaded one that teaches me about world maps instead. **Now:**

 A) I feel better about myself because I'm not comparing my life to my friends' lives.

AND

B) I know all the countries that make up Africa.

a Box', people who work there explain just how vital the things they learned in maths, science, history and other subjects have turned out to be when it came to making their films.

You can also learn skills that are specifically designed to help people. If you're as lucky as Cheng Yu-chung, they might be taught at your school. If not, why not check out some of those places I listed above?

One evening, sixteen-year-old Cheng was out jogging on the streets of Taipei, Taiwan,

when he came across an unconscious man named Tsai.

Luckily, Cheng had been taught CPR[1] when he was in primary school and he remembered what to do. Cheng immediately started performing CPR on Tsai until an ambulance showed up.

[1] This consists of repeating cycles of 30 chest compressions and two rescue breaths. If you've ever tried CPR on a dummy, you'll know it can be pretty exhausting, and Cheng ended up performing it for over 13 minutes.

Cheng didn't stop the CPR when the ambulance arrived. He continued to help the paramedics. It was Cheng's actions that saved the man's life, but he left the hospital without telling anyone who he was.

The fire department set about trying to trace him through the internet.

Eventually, someone on the internet recognised Cheng and got in contact with his father, who realised that it was his son who'd saved Tsai's life.

Cheng told the reporters who wanted to interview him that he was just a normal kid and that he didn't think what he'd done was a big deal. He couldn't believe the fire department were looking for him.

But it's not as easy as it sounds. I've completed a number of first-aid courses myself, the first when I was about eleven. Not long after that, I was with a friend when he accidentally cut his finger quite deeply with a craft knife. Blood started pouring from the wound. My friend turned pale and then passed out from the sight of the blood.

If it was as simple as remembering what I'd been told on a first-aid course, I could have jumped to his help. But instead I made a sound like a dog on bonfire night, put my hands on either side of my face and stood there in fear, not moving. (Don't worry, my friend's mum came to the rescue and he was fine in the end.)

But Cheng was able to keep calm, remember everything he'd learned and help someone in need. Being a hero, I realised, is not just about possessing knowledge, but about knowing how to use it. As I discovered then, when my friend was hurt, there is always more to learn.

Here's a game I sometimes like to play. If I was suddenly dropped back into medieval times, which things from today's world would I be able to make or introduce into their society? Could I introduce electricity? Would I be able to teach people about medicine? Could I show them how to broadcast radio? Would I even know how to make a good bowl of pasta? I'm not saying you **SHOULD** know all of those things. In fact, I know exactly none of those things. But it's a fun

game because it shows us just how much we have to learn, and how valuable learning these things can be. Socrates (a wise Greek philosopher) famously said that he didn't know anything. He said that this made him smarter than most people, as none of them realised that they knew nothing! Being aware of how little we know reminds us just how much we have to learn.

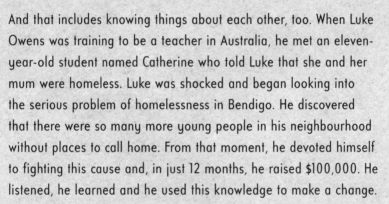

The more we know, the more we are capable of.

And that includes knowing things about each other, too. When Luke Owens was training to be a teacher in Australia, he met an eleven-year-old student named Catherine who told Luke that she and her mum were homeless. Luke was shocked and began looking into the serious problem of homelessness in Bendigo. He discovered that there were so many more young people in his neighbourhood without places to call home. From that moment, he devoted himself to fighting this cause and, in just 12 months, he raised $100,000. He listened, he learned and he used this knowledge to make a change.

There's a saying **'Knowledge is Power'**. And it's a kind of power you'll need if you're going to be a hero. Cheng's knowledge saved Tsai, Lizzie's saved Alex, Tilly's saved those people on the beach in Thailand and Luke's helped countless young homeless people. They each used information they had learned about the world and the people around them to do extraordinary things. So what are you going to go out and discover next?

7

'A TEACHER AFFECTS ETERNITY; HE CAN NEVER TELL WHERE HIS INFLUENCE STOPS.'
- Henry Adams.

One way you can be a hero is by helping people, another is by showing people how they can help themselves. We can't learn much at all without teachers. When I say teachers, I'm not just referring to those adults at school who tell you to stop picking your nose and put away your phone. Whether it's from authors, public speakers, journalists or documentary-makers, most of the things we know are taught to us by other people. We all become teachers too, at one point or another. Maybe you have younger siblings who need help tying their shoelaces. Maybe you have classmates who can't understand fractions as well as you. Or maybe your mum asks for your help when she's trying to upload pictures of the dog wearing sunglasses to Instagram. Regardless of how little you think you know, I guarantee that you've taught someone something.

No-one in this book would have been able to do any of the things they'd done had they not been taught by someone. But teaching is about much more than moving a fact from your head into someone else's.

Try asking one of your teachers why they do what they do. If they're anything like my teachers, they're there because they want to make a difference in the lives of the children they teach. The same can be said for Michael Wamaya.

Michael was just thirteen when his father died and he had to drop out of school to start earning money for his family. He mostly worked fixing cars and selling motor parts in Kenya.

One day Michael spotted a poster for the Kenya Performing Arts Group, inviting people to audition.

Michael decided to try it out. That was when he discovered ballet and his life changed.

Ballet gave Michael something to strive for. It allowed him to travel, to gain confidence, to dream and to see a future for himself, filled with meaning, hope and the joy of dance.

As he grew older, Michael wanted to give other children the chance that he had been given.

He founded a ballet school in Kibera, one of the poorest parts of Nairobi.

Many of his students have gone on to become accomplished dancers, a group of them even performed 'The Nutcracker' at the Kenya National Theatre.

'I teach because I believe that all children should have the opportunity of discovering their strengths. By allowing children the opportunity to learn, discover and develop themselves and their talents, we can change their perception of self-worth and they could become anything they want to be.'

Michael wanted a world where kids from poor neighbourhoods like his could flourish and express themselves through dance, so he went out and tried to build that world. That's what makes him a hero.

But it's not just ballet that can make such a difference in young people's lives. Here are just a few examples I've learned about that use teaching as a way of helping people:

In Paraguay, Favio Chavez created instruments from the rubbish of a massive dump, taught the children who lived there to play, and then organised them into an orchestra who have since played around the world.

Skateistan is a charity which teaches skateboarding to girls and boys in Afghanistan, South Africa and Cambodia, to empower kids to become leaders.

-The Turing Trust helps young people in Ghana and Malawi learn how to use computers, thus gaining skills and experience that can help them to flourish in a changing world.

-The Lightyear Foundation in the UK encourages children with disabilities to get involved with science, boosting their confidence and letting them know that they can get jobs in science, technology, engineering or mathematics.

Each of these examples shows just how powerful passing on your knowledge can be. When you teach someone something, you can end up giving them self-esteem, opportunities and hope. And it wasn't just the students that benefited from Michael's teaching. Starting his ballet school brought Michael joy, too.

By providing others with something that had given his so life so much happiness, he was living by the golden rule.

There is a quote by a sci-fi writer called Robert Heinlein which says,

'WHEN ONE TEACHES, TWO LEARN.'

He's saying that we learn by teaching others. We learn about ourselves, about other people, about the world and about our craft, whether it's ballet, writing, maths, or anything else.

Another person who set about trying to help others through education was a girl from America called Zuriel Oduwole.

At the age of nine, Zuriel entered a competition for young filmmakers.

Most of the other children made films about America. Zuriel decided to make hers about a revolution that had happened in Ghana, since both her parents had roots in Africa. She thought it was a subject not many people in her country would know much about.

Zuriel managed to secure a meeting with the former president of Ghana and she flew across the Atlantic Ocean to interview him for her film. While in Ghana, Zuriel met girls her age who were living on the streets and had no way of getting an education.

She wanted to share her knowledge with them. Zuriel started teaching young girls across Africa how to make films of their own. This way, they could share their own stories with the world, as well as making a living.

Zuriel was a hero because she shared her knowledge in two very important ways. In the first instance, she tried her best to teach other Americans about the tragedies affecting people in other parts of the world. In the second instance, she taught girls in Ghana, who had been born into more difficult circumstances, a way of expressing themselves, of telling their stories and of making money in order to become more independent.

Teachers can come in many forms. You could become a teacher right now – all you need to do is pass on a piece of information and allow others to benefit from your knowledge.

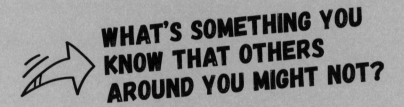

WHAT'S SOMETHING YOU KNOW THAT OTHERS AROUND YOU MIGHT NOT?

Maybe you know how to make scrambled eggs or draw horses or juggle. Maybe you've just learned something about the Romans or the Amazon Rainforest. Maybe you know the names of certain flowers, trees or birds.

Try passing on one piece of knowledge to someone you know, within the next twenty-four-hours. Though the effects might not be immediately obvious, you'll be surprised by how big they can be. When you give someone the gift of a fact, it can become something that they end up carrying with them throughout their entire lives.

One person who has shared their power with the rest of the world in a truly heroic way is Fiona Gameson.

Fiona Gameson became very unwell when she was just a baby. At eighteen months old, she lost the use of one eye. A year later, she lost the use of the other too.

From a young age, Fiona taught herself echolocation. She made a clicking sound with her mouth, listened to how it bounced off the objects around her and used this to create a mental map to navigate the world with.

It's the same technique that bats, whales and dolphins use.

Thanks to her skill at echolocation, Fiona can live a far more independent life than she might otherwise have done. She now teaches, lectures and holds workshops to try and teach other blind people about echolocation and show them how they can use it to navigate the world.

Fiona discovered something for herself and wanted to pass it on to those she thought might benefit from it. This sharing of knowledge is part of what makes us, as humans, such an amazing species. It's how we manage to stack up discoveries until we can create things that no one person could ever have done alone. Someone invents the wheel, for example, someone else invents the motor, other people invent red paint and airbags and reclining chairs, and the knowledge gets passed down until someone rearranges it into a Ferrari. If we didn't do this, every new generation of humans would have to learn to do everything for themselves.

One of the best examples of this is the website Wikipedia. You might have read an article on it if you've ever researched something online. Wikipedia is one of the biggest compendiums of human knowledge ever to have existed. As I'm writing this to you now, the English language version has over six million articles, with over 17,000 articles being added every month, read by 1.4 billion users in 300 different languages. Everyone shares the knowledge they have with the world, and it's all free. Wikipedia manages to grow so big because anyone can contribute, as long as they can back up the things they want to say. There's even a guide for younger users who want to start editing, and a section of the site called Wikipedia Teahouse where anyone can go for answers to questions they might have.

Sharing knowledge can often help people as much as sharing physical things. There's an old saying that I remember staring at for an hour every Tuesday and Friday at 11 o'clock (it was on a poster in the history classroom at school), it said:

'**GIVE** a man a fish, you'll feed him for a day.

TEACH a man to fish, you'll feed him for a lifetime.'

This sums up perfectly why teachers can be heroes. People like Zuriel or Fiona give others the skills that they need to gain their own freedom for a lifetime.

We should share knowledge to inspire and help each other.

One of the books I wrote before this one was called *Stories For Boys Who Dare to Be Different*. The aim of the book was to tell the stories of men who did amazing things despite not having qualities which society traditionally expects boys or men to have. So maybe they weren't big and strong, maybe they didn't play football or fight anyone, but each of them changed the world in their own way, whether it was through poetry, science or sheer kindness.

While looking for boys and men to include, I was inspired by a young boy named Christian McPhilamy. After hearing about how children with cancer could lose their hair, Christian decided to grow his hair, so it could be cut off and donated to a charity that made wigs. For two years, starting from the age of eight, Christian grew his blond hair. It wasn't easy. Other kids, and even adults, would make fun of him. But Christian ignored them. He knew how much a wig would mean to a child without hair.

A couple of weeks ago, while doing research for this book, I came across the story of a boy called Oliver Holmes, from England. Oliver had also decided to grow his hair so that he could cut it off and donate it to The Little Princess Trust charity. They make wigs for children who have lost their hair. When it was done, he even decided to shave his head completely, so he'd have some idea of how it feels for people who do lose their hair.

In the article, Oliver's mum said he'd been inspired to grow his hair after reading about Christian McPhilamy in *Stories for Boys Who Dare to Be Different*.

I'll admit, it's a nice feeling to realise that you're the tiny link between two very extraordinary people. It makes it worth remembering that if something inspires you, then it might well inspire other people, too.

This is one of the joys of sharing the things you've learned: you might nudge people to go in directions they may not otherwise have considered. You might make a difference in someone else's life and they might make a difference in someone else's life and that chain can go on forever.

We often overlook many of the people who play key roles in the world. Scientific breakthroughs are often credited to one person rather than a team or a long line of people working away at the same problem. In football, whoever scores the goal is remembered, even though they never would have touched the ball without the rest of their team.

But behind almost every story of success is a teacher of some kind.

A quick flick through this book will show you that. Everything that happens in the world is a team effort, no one can do anything alone. Some of the most important and life-changing ways that you can help other people involve sharing your knowledge and passing on the things you've learned.

IF YOU REALLY WANT
TO BE THE KIND OF
HERO WHO MAKES
A DIFFERENCE,
THEN GIVING
SOMEONE ELSE
THE GIFT OF
YOUR KNOWLEDGE
IS A GOOD
PLACE
TO START.

USE
WHAT
YOU HAVE

8

'TO ACHIEVE GREATNESS:
START WHERE YOU ARE.
USE WHAT YOU HAVE.
DO WHAT YOU CAN.'
— Arthur Ashe

We all have natural strengths. These strengths may be physical, they may be mental or they may be parts of your character. Michael Phelps, a famous American swimmer, for example, has size fourteen feet, lungs twice as large as the average human and a wingspan that makes him wider than he is tall. These natural advantages, together with a whole lot of training, meant that it was possible for him to become not just one of the best swimmers of all time, but the athlete with the most Olympic medals in history – 28!

Bill Gates, on the other hand, has described himself as an introvert who likes spending time alone. Without that aspect to his personality, I can't imagine he would have spent so much of his teenage years staring at a computer screen. And if he hadn't devoted himself to those machines, he may never have founded Microsoft and become one of the richest men in the world.

There is, however, no strength that is not sometimes a weakness. There are also many things that can appear as weaknesses in some situations but can prove incredibly useful in others. Being the size of Michael Phelps is no help at all if you want to be a horse rider, a Formula One driver or the owner of a crowded shop filled with delicate antiques. While being as introverted as Bill Gates might be more of a hindrance than a help if, instead of creating computer systems, you were trying to perform at a concert, lead a team of construction workers or serve customers in a busy restaurant.

Someone once said:
EVERYBODY IS A GENIUS.
But if you judge a fish by its ability to climb a tree, it will live its whole life believing that it is stupid.

What this means is that we all have things we're good at, but if you judge us by the things we're not able to do then well always feel like failures. Michael Phelps looks impressive when you see him tearing his way across an Olympic swimming pool, but if you sat him on a horse, asked him to sing an Ariana Grande song, or invited him to help a team of archaeologists on a dig, he might start to look like a fish trying to climb a tree.

TRY JOTTING DOWN A FEW OF YOUR STRENGTHS AND WEAKNESSES.

They can be absolutely anything. Write down whatever comes to mind, as big or small as you like, but try to keep the list balanced, so that there aren't more weaknesses than strengths or strengths than weaknesses.

Now I want you to find ways of rewriting some of your weaknesses so that you can slide them across to the strengths column. Are there certain situations where those things might help you or other people? Are there some ways in which they might be useful? **I'll try first.**

⚡ One of my weaknesses is being shy – a strength of this is that I've found other ways to express myself (writing, painting, recording painfully loud songs about my favourite foods).

⚡ Another of my weaknesses is that I'm incredibly restless and impatient – a strength of this is that I have a lot of energy that can be used to make many different things.

It is up to us to find our strengths and it is up to us how we decide to use them. Sometimes, we already know what our strengths are. Sometimes they might make themselves known in the most unusual ways.

Joy Milne first met her husband, Les, when they were in school. They fell in love, got married, had children and both found jobs working in hospitals. Neither of them would have guessed that Joy had one of the strangest and most amazing natural strengths anyone had ever heard of.

One day, Les came home and Joy noticed that he smelled different. She asked him to shower but the smell didn't go away. Some time later, Joy started to notice that it wasn't just her husband's smell that was changing. His personality changed too. Over ten years after she first noticed the smell, Les was diagnosed with a disease called Parkinson's disease.[1]

[1] Parkinson's disease is an illness which damages the brain.

At a support group for people with the disease, Joy realised that all of the other people with Parkinson's smelled different too. When Joy told a scientist she thought she could smell Parkinson's, he didn't believe her.[1]

But they ran tests where Joy had to sniff people and say whether she thought they had the disease or not. She got every single one right, except for one man. Not long after the experiment, the man called to say he'd just been diagnosed with the disease. Joy had been right all along.

Joy has since been working with researchers from all around the world to try and use her superpower to help create a reliable, early test for the disease.

[1] It's like saying 'I can smell a broken arm' or 'I can smell a headache'!

Unfortunately, there isn't a cure for Parkinson's yet, but there are ways of slowing it down. And, thanks to Joy's efforts, many families might soon be able to know well in advance that the disease is coming, so that they can prepare.

When Joy realised that she had a very rare gift, a strength that no-one else in the world seemed to have, she was determined to use it to try and help other families in a similar position to her. Like a hero, Joy fought to help others even at such a difficult time for herself. There's a big chance Joy could have gone through life never realising she had a strength that could help so many people. It just shows how many talents and abilities we might possess without even knowing.

How could you ever discover that you had a talent for handstands if you never tried to do one? What about writing poems, designing houses or cooking? There are so many things that we may never discover our passions or talents for, simply because we never try them.

So let's start now!

Choose at least two ideas from this list and give them a go. It doesn't matter if none of them are things you're familiar with, this is about trying something new:

FIND three balls or apples or rolled-up socks and use them to try and learn juggling.

DESIGN your dream house. You could even look at some architectural plans online.

PLOT your own expedition around the world. Where would you go? Why? How would you get there?

WRITE a poem about a time you felt amazed. You could even try submitting it to a competition.

BAKE cookies using a recipe. Can you add a couple of extra ingredients of your own?

ARRANGE for your friends or family to get together and play Ultimate Frisbee (you can find the rules online.) If you enjoy it, there are clubs and competitions in most countries throughout the world.

LEARN a character's speech from a play, film or TV show and perform it for someone.

RECORD a wildlife documentary.[1] Do some research on the animals you're filming so you can give it an interesting voiceover.

MAKE some calculations about your life. How many minutes have you spent brushing your teeth in your life so far? How many eggs have you eaten in total? How many times have you laughed?

CHOOSE an object in your house and go on a research mission to discover how it works. How does a toaster toast bread? How do kettles boil water?

[1] If you don't have something to record this on, you could ask someone in your family if you can borrow their phone or camera.

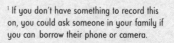

They might sound like silly challenges, but you never know what might spark an interest or uncover a talent. You could be surprised by the strengths you already have within you and how useful they can turn out to be.

Someone else who wanted to use his natural ability to help others was an Australian man named James Harrison. When James was fourteen, he had to be admitted to hospital for surgery. His life was saved by blood that someone had donated. Once he'd recovered, James pledged to start donating blood as soon and as often as he could.

Doctors soon realised that there was something very special about James' blood. It contained unique antibodies that could fight a disease called Rhesus.

Doctors used James' blood to make a medication called Anti-D which could cure Rhesus disease. To help them in their efforts, James started giving blood plasma almost every week of his life. Every single dose of this medicine came from James' blood.

At the age of 81, James gave his last blood donation.[1] It is thought that James may have impacted up to two million lives. Even his own daughter was given the medicine made from his blood.

Like Joy, James found himself with a unique strength. He didn't choose the ability, but he did choose to

[1] 81 is the maximum legal age that someone can donate blood in Australia.

use it for good. He decided, week after week, to go and donate his blood plasma. He didn't want to let his superpower go to waste.

OUR STRENGTHS may prove useful but we shouldn't feel limited by them. Just because someone like Michael Phelps has a few natural advantages, it doesn't mean that someone without those advantages can't measure up to them.

At the 100m butterfly race in the 2016 Olympics, Michael was beaten by a virtually unknown swimmer from Singapore named Joseph Schooling. Joseph was shorter than Michael, lighter than Michael and ten years younger than Michael. He not only beat the legendary swimmer, but he set a new Olympic record and earned the first ever Olympic medal for his country, too.

You can't change the size of your feet but you can choose how much you work at something, how you spend your time and how you apply yourself. Often people decide that if they don't have certain strengths now, then they'll never have them. One of the common ways this might appear in school is people saying 'I'm just not good at maths' or 'I've never really been able to do languages.' But neither of those things are fixed. Our brains, unlike our feet, change depending on what we do with them. The more maths you do, the better you'll become.

When I was eleven, I was put in the bottom set for maths, along with one of my best friends. Neither of us could get our heads around much when it came to numbers. Most of the time, we sat near the back of the class and talked about computer games and what we were going to eat at breaktime (usually a bag of chocolate chips or a giant swiss roll).

One year, my friend got told off by his parents for his low maths grades. After that, he started asking our teacher questions and listening to the answers. He started actually doing his homework too, rather than hurriedly copying off someone else right before the lesson started.

Not long after that, he was bumped up to a better set. I was left alone in the bottom set, cutting notches into the plastic tables with my ruler and wondering when the bell would go, so I could get out of the classroom and see my friend again.

At the end of our last year at school, my friend took the advanced maths exams. To me it looked as complicated as those equations scientists do in films when they're trying to figure out time travel. He went off to study something very serious, complicated and mathsy at university.

Clearly, my friend had the potential to excel at maths all along, he just hadn't realised it. He assumed that he was just bad at maths and always would be. When he was forced to try, he found that he had the ability to grasp the complicated ideas all along. (Remember earlier when I had to work out how long it would take everyone on earth to know they were great, if three people told three people each day? He was the one who worked that out when I couldn't!)

You may, if you're lucky, find yourself with incredibly large feet and a desire to win swimming competitions. If you're slightly less lucky, you might find yourself with tiny feet and the same desire. But big feet aren't the only strength you need to succeed at swimming. Maybe you have dedication. Maybe you have passion. Maybe you have the ability to get into a pool every day and train until your body feels like it's going to explode.

Our superpowers are not always obvious but that doesn't mean they're any less useful. Maybe you don't have rare blood or a magic nose, but you have the ability to stay positive even when things seem awful, the patience to explain things to others, or the focus to work on something for hour after hour without getting distracted.

Wolverine has razor-sharp claws, Thor has super-strength and Flash can move faster than the speed of light. But Batman has no superpowers. None at all. Every power of Batman's is something he learned for himself. Like my friend in maths, Batman had to work hard to develop his strengths. But that ability to work hard proved to be a strength in itself.

A hero might be born
with a power.
A hero might
develop a power.
**WHAT MATTERS IS ONLY
THAT A HERO USES THEIR
POWER FOR GOOD.**

9

'STAND UP FOR WHAT IS RIGHT, EVEN IF YOU STAND ALONE.'
- Suzy Kassem

We all have beliefs about right and wrong. I don't, for example, generally think it's okay to hit people. I also don't think you should ever drink milk straight from the bottle, take your socks off on an aeroplane or tell people the endings to films they haven't seen yet. These beliefs weren't there the day I was born, they grew over time, the more I got to know about other people and myself. They came from discovering things and from imagining the kind of world I would like to live in.

Most of us also have beliefs about how people deserve to be treated. For example, if one of your friends was caught talking during a maths lesson, you might believe it's right that they get some kind of punishment. After all, if there were no repercussions for talking, everyone would talk all the time, no-one would learn anything and I wouldn't have a friend who could help me work out how long it would take for everyone in the world to be told they're great.

If, however, the teacher decided to take your friend's lunch money as punishment for talking, you might believe that they're being completely unreasonable. Of course the friend shouldn't have been chatting but it's not right to deprive them of food because of it.

When you see something that you believe is wrong or unfair, you could choose to say nothing. Or you could choose to stand up for that belief, to explain why you think it's wrong, and to try and change things.

Quite often, it's difficult to stand up for our beliefs, even when we see things that feel unjust. It can be difficult for all kinds of reasons. Sometimes it's difficult because it involves standing up to someone bigger, older or with more power than us. Sometimes it's difficult because the thing you're standing up against has existed for a long time. Other times it's difficult because no-one else is doing it.

Although it may feel too hard or lonely at first, good causes have a way of gaining momentum. Take the example of **Greta Thunberg**, who started her fight against climate change alone outside a government building with a hand-painted sign. As more and more people heard her message, more and more children turned out to join her. Now Greta is responsible for a wave of protests involving millions of children from all around the world.

A hero like Greta is someone whose actions match their beliefs. (These have to be good beliefs, of course, not beliefs like: *I should be king of the universe* or *everyone should give me the best parts of their packed lunches.*)

They have an idea of the kind of world they want to live in and that is the kind of world they set out to create.

Imagine you're a superhero. I'm not sure what your power is, you can decide. Perhaps you're The Human Tree and can shoot leaves from your hands, or Maths Man, and you can pose problems so difficult that they freeze people with confusion. (Whatever your power is, you hold the belief that it is wrong for people to take things that don't belong to them.) One day you're driving around, when you see a robber trying to steal someone's bag. This goes completely against what you believe is right. So you hop out of your car and start using whatever power you have to separate the criminal from the victim.

If you didn't do anything to stop the attacker and just drove on, then negative thoughts would start to consume you. Why didn't I do anything? you'd think. What kind of superhero am I? I knew what was happening was wrong but I ignored it. I didn't stand up for what I believed in.

This might be an exaggerated example but the message is the same – you should always try and match your behaviour to your beliefs, to stand up for what you think is right.

And it's never too soon to start fighting for the causes you care about.

Isabel and Melati Wijsen are sisters who grew up on the island of Bali. They loved their home but hated the sight of its beautiful beaches and blue waters being covered with plastic rubbish. At the ages of ten and twelve, the sisters decided they would start campaigning for plastic bags to be completely banned on the island.

Isabel and Melati collected over one hundred thousand signatures, to show the local government how passionate everyone was about this issue. They then organised over twelve thousand volunteers to come together and clean up the beaches.

The sisters even went on a hunger strike, fasting between sunrise and sunset each day. Eventually, four years after they started their campaign, plastic bags were completely banned in Bali.

'We didn't want to wait until it was too late to stand up for what we believe in.'

By not waiting, they managed to make a real change.

It's a daunting prospect, trying to tackle such big problems when you're so young. But Isabel and Melati are proof that you can make a difference. No matter how small you may be, there's a way of making your voice heard. The girls did what none of the politicians seemed to want to do: they stood up for what they believed in and took action.

It took years of campaigning, not just by the Wijsen sisters, but by many other people too, before the government were finally convinced to make a change.

HEROES line their beliefs up **WITH THEIR ACTIONS.**

Someone else who got frustrated that the adults in charge weren't doing enough for the planet was Felix Finkbeiner, a nine-year-old boy from Germany. One day, Felix was asked to give a presentation to his class about climate change.

During his research, Felix came across the story of Wangari Maathai from Kenya.

Wangari had fought against the destruction of forests in her country. She had planted over thirty million trees in an attempt to combat climate change.

WANGARI MAATHAI

Felix couldn't understand why adults weren't doing more to protect the planet like Wangari had done.

Inspired by Wangari's story, he decided to launch a campaign called Plant-for-the-Planet, to try and get one million children to plant a total of one million trees in each country on Earth.

Three years after starting, they reached this goal. Felix spoke around the world and started growing his organisation. It soon became a huge network of children and young people, spread across 74 countries, all fighting the climate crisis by reforesting different corners of the earth.

Today, Felix is twenty-two and he still runs Plant-for-the-Planet. They've planted nearly fourteen billion trees, which is two trees for every single person in the world. Their new aim? One trillion.

Both the Wijsen sisters and Felix used direct action to achieve their goals. They spotted something they didn't like and set out trying to change it.

It's easy not to notice what's happening around you sometimes. Often we get so wrapped up in our lives, that we barely know what's happening in our own homes, let alone in the world.

We also tend **TO MISS** the things we aren't looking for.

Take this example:

In 2004, Daniel Simons and Christopher Chabris decided to conduct an experiment. They showed their test subjects a video of people passing a basketball back and forth. The test subjects had to count the number of passes made between the players.

At the end, Daniel and Christopher asked the subjects if they'd seen anything unusual about the video. Over half said they didn't. But there *was* something unusual about the video: halfway through, a woman in a full gorilla suit walked directly through the shot, past the players who were passing the ball. It's pretty hard to miss. If you don't believe me, go on YouTube and watch the video for yourself. 'How could anyone have missed that?' you'll think.

They missed the gorilla because they hadn't been looking for it. They didn't expect it and so they didn't notice it.

And if people can miss a gorilla wandering across a basketball court, then it's easy to imagine how you might miss something important, right in front of you, like someone looking a little upset. So it's worth looking around you sometimes.

Is there something happening in your school that you don't think is right? What about your country? Or the planet?

There are ways that you can get involved with even the biggest and most daunting causes. Plant-for-the-Planet are always looking for young people who want to get involved. The website change.org has thousands of important petitions you can sign. And the human rights charity Amnesty International has a section of its website devoted to helping you send letters or emails to the people in charge about important issues or causes.

One letter may not make a difference, but one million can't be ignored. However, you don't always need to stand up for things in such direct ways.

A protest doesn't always have to involve marching around the streets holding a placard or sending letters to your government (as effective as those things can be). Sometimes a protest can mean creating a work of art. Famous artists throughout history have used their work to draw attention to injustices:

⚡ The folk singer **BOB DYLAN** once wrote a protest song called 'Hurricane'. It drew attention to a man named Rubin Carter, who was in prison for a crime he didn't commit. Because of the song, Rubin was given another trial.

⚡ After hearing that a small town named Guernica had been bombed to ruins during the Second World War, **PABLO PICASSO** painted a vast and heart-breaking painting. The artwork, which is called *Guernica*, travelled the world as a warning about the destruction and devastation of war.

⚡ At a time when slavery was still legal in many parts of the USA, **HARRIET BEECHER-STOWE** wrote a novel called *Uncle Tom's Cabin*. It portrayed the pain and suffering of people who had been kidnapped from their homelands, treated as property and forced to be slaves. The year it was published, the Bible was the only book that sold more copies than Harriet's novel.

⚡ In protest of how his government treated art and artists, **AI WEIWEI** once photographed himself smashing a 2000-year-old Chinese vase worth over one million dollars. Ai wanted to show the world how painful it was to watch the way his government was treating its citizens.

Though their names are now known by many people around the world, Bob, Pablo, Harriet and Ai were also just ordinary people with remarkable talents. They used what they were good at to raise awareness of things they were passionate about. **They wanted to change the world with their art. Like the other heroes in this book, they decided to stand up for their beliefs and make our planet a better place.**

To be a hero, you do not have to embark on a relentless mission to right every wrong in the world, but you should try to make sure that your actions match your beliefs. If you think bullying is wrong, say something when you come across it. If you think we should all be doing our bit to fight climate change, then try your best not to waste water or electricity.

To continue on your journey of becoming a superhero, try to come up with three causes that you care about. They can be big or small, local or international, something you already know about or something you haven't yet learned much about at all. The causes can involve anything, including poverty, disease, education, animals, human rights, natural disasters, racism, sexism and any other area in which people are in need of help and support.

Now do some research into how you might get involved with those causes. You don't have to do something huge, even sharing your knowledge about a cause with someone else can be helpful. What's important is that you find a way of standing up for what you believe in, no matter how small the stand you take might be.

'EVERY DECISION WE MAKE IS A VOTE WE ARE CASTING FOR THE TYPE OF WORLD IN WHICH WE WANT TO LIVE.'

– Crispin Best

If you can find the determination to fight for your beliefs, you'll be able to help build the kind of world you want to live in. A world where the oceans aren't filled with plastic bags, where trees cover the surface of the earth, and where we all start noticing the gorillas standing right in front of us. If you can do that, you're a hero to me. A hero, after all, is anyone who wants to live in a better world and decides to do something about it.

10

'IMAGINATION WILL OFTEN CARRY US TO WORLDS THAT NEVER WERE. BUT WITHOUT IT WE GO NOWHERE.'
- Carl Sagan

We don't live in a perfect world. Orange juice splashes when you pour it from the carton, dodos have been hunted to extinction and millions of cars belch black smoke into the atmosphere. There are lots of things about life on Earth that are imperfect.

And there are also lots of people who want to make things that will change that.

One of the best pieces of advice I've ever read came from an inspiring American writer named Toni Morrison. She said: 'If the book you want to read doesn't exist, then you have to write it.' But this isn't just true of books. If there's anything that you wish exists but doesn't yet, then you should try and make it a reality.

Let's go right back to the beginning of the book, to dreaming big and letting your mind wander to all the possibilities the future holds.

When you dream of your future, you sit and ask yourself, what if ...
What if I become a doctor without borders? What if I sail around the
world alone? What if I become a clown and bring joy to as many
people as possible?

But a hero can also turn these 'what ifs' outwards to the world.
Instead of asking yourself what you could turn *yourself* into, you
can ask what kind of place you can turn the world into.

What if we lived in a world where the ocean was free of plastic?

What if we lived on a planet where everyone had access to clean water?

And what if there was a food so delicious that while you ate it, you forgot about every worry you ever had?

Anirudh Sharma was exactly the kind of person who dared to wonder 'what if...'

The World Health Organization states that air pollution is one of the biggest threats to humans. Yet, most of the time, we barely notice it.[1]

While walking in Mumbai, India, Anirudh saw this first-hand. He watched black smoke bellowing out of cars, motorbikes and buses.

Back at home, Anirudh had an idea.

[1] Except if you pick your nose after riding the London Underground, in which case you may well find your bogeys have gone black.

He got a team together and created a product called kaalink.

Kaalink could be fitted to a car exhaust pipe, where it would collect the fumes that would otherwise have been pumped into the air.

But kaalink didn't just collect the exhaust fumes, it turned them into:

INK

NYC

DONUTS
CENTRAL PARK

TAXI

THIS ART IS PAINTED
WITH AIR POLLUTION

Anirudh has since travelled around the world, challenging artists who live in smoke-filled cities to create beautiful works of art using this special ink.

Anirudh's creation isn't just helping to save the environment and protect our health, it's also giving artists the tools to create works of real beauty.

LOOKING AT THE WORLD
AND SEEING
HOW HARMFUL THINGS
can be turned into
something beautiful
ISN'T AN EASY TASK.

In fact, before hearing stories like this, it's something I would have dismissed as impossible. People being able to see possibilities like this is how we have managed to go from wandering hunter-gatherers, dressed in furs, to people with microwaves, boats and Peppa Pig. People like Anirudh can see the endless possibilities inside lumps of clay or logs or car exhaust fumes. To them, the world is like a giant set of Lego which they can rearrange. **They are heroes because they refuse to accept the world as it is. Instead, they seek to change things in a way that makes life better for everyone else.**

Kelvin Doe also started rearranging the world for the better from a very young age.

Kelvin was born in Freetown, Sierra Leone.

He lived in a poor area where the electricity would sometimes only come on once a week,

only to disappear again soon after, plunging homes into darkness.

At the age of ten, Kelvin began searching through scrap,

hunting for pieces of metal and old electronic devices.

He taught himself how they worked, how they could be brought back to life and how they could fit together.

When Kelvin was thirteen, he used this scrap to build a battery capable of powering his home and the homes around it.

Then, to bring his community together, Kelvin also built a radio and recording equipment from scrap, and started his own radio show.

After hearing about his work, the famous Massachusetts Institute of Technology in America invited Kelvin to conduct research there.[1] Kelvin now lives and studies in Canada, where he's running a project that aims to support young innovators in Sierra Leone and around the world. He hopes to return soon, so that he can show the next generation that even if something doesn't exist, they can make it themselves.

[1] At sixteen, he was the youngest person ever to have been invited.

By refusing to accept the way things were, Kelvin made a big difference in the lives of the people around him. He wouldn't accept that the electricity just didn't stay on. He wouldn't accept that there was no community radio station for his neighbourhood. He had a vision of the way the world could be, and he worked hard to make this happen. Kelvin's inventions improved the lives of his family and neighbours, and he's continuing to inspire more people today. That is why he's a hero.

You never know what effect an invention might have on the world. It might light up a community. It might bring people together. Or it might end up bringing joy to millions of people around the world.

Some inventions have obvious benefits. Of course seatbelts and X-rays and lifejackets are important. But many other things that were invented by ordinary people have played a part in making life rich, interesting and joyful.

NOT EVERY HERO SAVES LIVES, SOME OF THEM JUST BRING SMILES TO OUR FACES. AND THAT SHOULD NOT BE UNDERESTIMATED.

Ruth Graves Wakefield was a teacher in Massachusetts in the 1920s. When she quit her job, she and her husband decided to buy an old toll house and turn it into a restaurant.

The restaurant soon became known for two things: its lobster dinners and Ruth's desserts.

TOLL HOUSE
Luncheons Dinners

One day, when Ruth was baking cookies for the guests, she realised she'd run out of baker's chocolate.[1] Ruth decided to cut up a bar of Nestle regular chocolate instead and scatter the pieces into her mixture. She thought they'd just end up melting into the cookies like the baking chocolate did.

They didn't. The lumps of chocolate stayed whole. And the cookies were all the more delicious for it. The Toll House cookies became famous, and people came to taste them from far and wide.

In fact, they're still popular today. Although we now just call them chocolate chip cookies.

Mmm Everybody's Making TOLL HOUSE COOKIES

[1] Baker's chocolate is different to normal chocolate, because it melts completely when baked.

I doubt that Ruth would have called herself a hero. But I've lost count of the number of times that I've had a truly awful day improved by a cup of tea and a few (an entire packet of) chocolate chip cookies. (I'm not really supposed to encourage you to eat chocolate chip cookies, but I will say that munching celery tends not to make me quite as happy.)

It can take a lot of courage to try something new. Whether it's devoting yourself to an invention or attempting something that's never been done before, heading out into the unknown is always going to be scary. But if you're not happy with the way the world is, then the unknown is where you have to go. Because the unknown is where you can make the greatest discoveries. The unknown is where heroes dare to venture in search of a better future.

When I sat down to start writing this book, the bright white screen on my computer was terrifying. I didn't know how to start. I didn't know how to carry on. I didn't know if everything I typed was going to sound so stupid that nobody would even want to waste paper printing it. Let's just use the paper as loo roll instead, they might have said. I'd rather wipe my bottom with it than ruin it with his silly sentences.

But it was a book I wanted to read and it didn't exist yet. So I started writing. And I wrote about all the incredible people I'd come across, people who aren't any different to you or me, except that they found their own ways of making life on our pale blue dot a little bit better. I'm not trying to say that I'm a hero for writing this, even though it did involve a heroic amount of sitting still and having to delete several computer games, but **I do know how scary it can be to start something from nothing and bring one of your ideas into the world.**

WHAT IS A SUPERHERO?

Before we both get back to our lives, I want to tell you the story of one more hero. He is as much of a hero as any of the other people in this book, though he'd be pretty confused to find himself on these pages. I've decided to include him here because he probably could have slotted into any one of the other chapters.

As a teenager, Richard Stanton saw a programme on TV called *The Underground Eiger*. It followed two cave divers as they made a record-breaking 6,000-feet dive into a cave in North Yorkshire.

Richard was entranced. That, he decided, was what he wanted to do. At university, Richard joined the caving club and the diving club. He taught himself to dive in the waters of Lancaster's River Lune.

For most of his life, Richard worked as a fireman, but continued cave diving in his spare time. Over many years, Richard built up a reputation

of being an incredible diver. He could go where many others couldn't, stay calm in cramped conditions and lead a team through the dark tunnels of the world's deepest caves.

In 2018, a football team of twelve boys and their coach became trapped in a cave in Thailand. The whole world watched on nervously as rescue attempts were made. If the boys couldn't be reached in time, their oxygen would run out. But the complex network of flooded caves and tunnels made them almost impossible to reach.

For an entire week, no-one could make contact with the boys.

Richard and his diving partner, John Volanthen, dropped everything they were doing and flew to Thailand to help. They were known as two of the best divers in the world.

Ten days after the boys disappeared, Richard and John finally found them. Getting them out was a race against time that would involve over ten thousand people, two thousand soldiers, ten helicopters, seven ambulances and one billion litres of water being pumped out the cave.

two Thai divers, Saman Kunan and Beirut Pakbara, died on But, thanks to Richard and John, all of the young survived.

s from the cave, **Richard told reporters st had a very specific set of skills that n hobby.**

But I think that's exactly what a hero is. Someone who uses their particular skills, passions or knowledge to do what they can for the people around them. Someone who finds a beneficial way of fitting into the world. Someone like Richard Stanton.

People like Richard prove that it is possible to use the thing you love to give something back to the world. It is possible to follow your own path and still find your superpower. It is possible for everyone to find ways, however big or small, of becoming a hero.

If I'm honest, by writing this book I've come to see how much more I could be doing. I don't mean that I feel guilty about not doing enough, just that I want to do more.

I want to engage more with other people, to form connections and to learn and teach.

I want to find new dreams, rekindle old ones and discover new talents.

I want to stop comparing myself to other people.

I want to create things, stand up for what I believe in and support the things that I care about.

MOST OF ALL, I JUST WANT TO DO A BIT OF GOOD.

The point of this book was never to make anyone feel bad for not doing as much as other people. It was to prove that by doing things for others, we can improve our own lives as well as theirs. We become healthier and happier and end up existing in a world that looks more like the kind of place we all want to live in.

A hero doesn't have to wear a cape, defeat evil villains or throw themselves into dangerous situations. A hero just has to make the world a slightly better place than they found it. This might be by being a kind and supportive friend, writing stories that spread important messages, painting a neighbourhood, inventing new dishes or saving people in danger. I don't know what your skills, talents or passions are, all I know is that I hope you find some way of turning them into a superpower. I hope I've also managed to prove to you that heroes are not just those villain-fighting, wall-climbers we meet in comics and films. And, most importantly, **that not all heroes wear capes.**

At the beginning of this book, we decided that a hero is anyone who wants to live in a better world and decides to do something about it. Since then, we've met lots of people who fit perfectly into that definition. The only questions left are:

DO YOU WANT TO LIVE IN A BETTER WORLD?

CAN YOU MAKE A DIFFERENCE?

AND ARE YOU READY TO FIND YOUR POWER AND DO SOMETHING EXTRAORDINARY?

REFERENCES

Page 4. *Batman: The Dark Knight Rises.* Warner Bros Pictures, DC Entertainment, Legendary Pictures, Syncopy, 2012.

Page 9. Vincent Peale, Norman. *The Power of Positive Thinking.* (Prentice Hall, 1952)

Page 23. Waldo Emerson, Ralph. *Essays: First Series.* (Prviately published, 1841)

Page 39. Viscott, David. *Finding Your Strength in Difficult Times: A Book of Meditations.* (Contemporary Books, 1993)

Page 42. Hreljac, Ryan. 2014. Interview with Ryan Hreljac. Accessed 28 October 2020. https://myhero.com/RYAN_HRELJAC

Page 55. Nimoy, Leonard. *These Words Are For You.* (Blue Mountain Arts, 1981)

Page 83. Transcript of speech. Yousafzai, Malala. 2013. https://www.theguardian.com/commentisfree/2013/jul/12/malala-yousafzai-united-nations-education-speech-text

Page 97. Adams, Henry. T*he Education of Henry Adams.* (Privately published, 1907)

Page 99. Wamaya, Michæl. Global Teacher Prize. Accessed 28 October 2020. https://www.globalteacherprize.org/person?id=2736

Page 101. Heinlein, Robert. *The Green Hills of Earth.* (Buccaneer Books, 1990)

Page 113. Arthur Ashe Quotes. BrainyQuote.com, BrainyMedia Inc, 2020. https://www.brainyquote.com/quotes/arthur_ashe_371527, accessed November 10, 2020

Page 125. Kassem, Suzy. *Rise Up and Salute the Sun.* (Awakened Press, 2011)

Page 137. Best, Crispin. 'How Good'. *Hello.* (Partus Press, 2019)

Page 139. Sagan, Carl. *Cosmos.* (Random House, 1980)

RESOURCES

Amnesty International
The world's largest grassroots organisation dedicated to protecting human rights:
https://www.amnesty.org.uk/

Appopo
A charity that trains animals to find landmines and tuberculosis: **https://www.apopo.org/en**

Change.org
A website for people to start campaigns and sign petitions for causes they care about:
https://www.change.org/

Coursera
A website with hundreds of online courses, certifications and degrees in a huge range of
subjects: **https://www.coursera.org/**

edX
A website that hosts online university-level courses in a wide range of subjects:
https://www.edx.org/

Ellen MacArthur Foundation
A charity that aims to build a circular economy for the future:
https://www.ellenmacarthurfoundation.org

The Khan Academy
A non-profit educational organisation that provides online tools, lessons, videos and materials
to help educate students: **https://www.khanacademy.org/**

The Lightyear Foundation
Encourages children with disabilities to get involved with science, technology, maths and
engineering: **https://www.lightyearfoundation.org/**

Little Princess Trust
A trust providing wigs to children with hair loss: **https://www.lightyearfoundation.org/**

NHS Charities Together
Charities supporting NHS staff and volunteers caring for COVID-19 patients:
https://www.nhscharitiestogether.co.uk/

Pay It Forward Day
A global initiative to create a huge ripple of kindness: **http://payitforwardday.com**

Plant for the Planet Ryan's Well Foundation
A charitable organisation dedicated to providing solutions to the water crisis in developing
countries: **https://www.ryanswell.ca/**

Save the Rhino
A charity working to conserve all five rhino species: **https://www.savetherhino.org**

Skateistan
A non-profit organisation empowering children through skateboarding and education in Afghanistan,
Cambodia and South Africa: **https://skateistan.org/**

SOS Children's Villages
A charity dedicated to caring for children who have lost one or both parents:
https://www.soschildrensvillages.org.uk/

The Turing Trust
An organisation that reuses computers and teaches Information Technology to communities in
Sub-Saharan Africa: **https://turingtrust.co.uk/**

Wikipedia
An online encyclopaedia created and maintained by a community of volunteer editors:
https://www.wikipedia.org/

Youtube
An online video sharing platform, where users can upload, view, rate, share, comment and
subscribe to videos and other users: **https://www.youtube.com/**

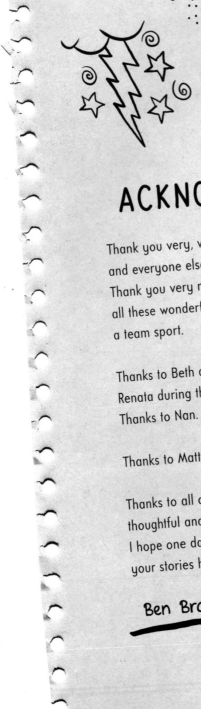

ACKNOWLEDGEMENTS

Thank you very, very much to Phoebe, Debbie, Tina, Laura and everyone else at Wren & Rook for all their hard work. Thank you very much to Nigel too, whose illustrations brought all these wonderful people to life. Making books is very much a team sport.

Thanks to Beth and Guy for putting up with me and Renata during the weird time over which this was written. Thanks to Nan. Good luck to Crispy and Little Crispy.

Thanks to Matthew Hamilton. And to Jan and Katy.

Thanks to all of the people who did the kind, brave, thoughtful and powerful things that made this book possible. I hope one day to meet you all and tell you just how much your stories have inspired me

Ben Brooks